I0804898

Fort Halifax

Winslow's Historic Outpost

Daniel J. Tortora

THE History PRESS

Published by The History Press
Charleston, SC 29403
www.historypress.net

Copyright © 2014 by Daniel J. Tortora
All rights reserved

Front cover, top: Major General Winslow's plan for Fort Halifax, 1754. *Adapted from a 1754 map reprinted in 1912 by the Massachusetts Historical Society.*
Bottom: Fort Halifax, by H.A. "Rudy" Fougere, 1997. *Winslow Public Library.*

Back cover, top: Bea White, Priscilla McKallip and Grace Towle prepare the blockhouse for the Maine DAR Field Day, July 11, 1954. *Fort Halifax Chapter, DAR.*
Bottom: Fort Halifax, 2012. *Author photo.*

First published 2014

Manufactured in the United States

ISBN 978.1.62619.292.8

Library of Congress CIP data applied for.

Notice: The information in this book is true and complete to the best of our knowledge. It is offered without guarantee on the part of the author or The History Press. The author and The History Press disclaim all liability in connection with the use of this book.

All rights reserved. No part of this book may be reproduced or transmitted in any form whatsoever without prior written permission from the publisher except in the case of brief quotations embodied in critical articles and reviews.

Contents

Acknowledgements

This book is the byproduct of the knowledge, support and kindness offered by numerous individuals from Winslow, Waterville, Colby College and beyond.

Members of the Winslow community were generous with their time and expertise and made this project all the more special. The staff at the Winslow Town Office, including town manager Mike Heavener, allowed me to sift through reports and meeting minutes. Winslow Parks and Recreation provided access to the blockhouse. Pam Bonney, director of the Winslow Public Library, opened up the library's collections. Gerry Poissonier, Elery Keene and the Friends of Fort Halifax shared stories, correspondence and good cheer. Tom McCowan of the Winslow Historical Preservation Committee provided scans of historic images. Jack Nivison offered his experiences in the flood of 1987, his sharp memory and an extensive contact list and also helped with research. Stan Mathieu recalled his decades-long commitment to the blockhouse and contributed slides, photos and historical knowledge. Rudy Fougere provided his sketches and insights. Interviews with present and former Winslow residents Pearley Lachance, Lee Spaulding, John Giroux and Steve Clark proved essential to Chapter 7. Roland Lessard, Jo Ann Nivison, Janice Mathieu and Brenda Poissonier made my research trips more fun.

In Waterville, Scott Monroe, managing editor of the *Morning Sentinel*, offered access to files and photos that I could not have done without. The Fort Halifax Chapter, DAR, and its regent, Barbara Healy, shared scrapbooks and family histories, helping me fill in gaps in the narrative.

Acknowledgements

I am indebted to David K. Thomas and Colin Hull, Colby College Class of 2015, for their patience and persistence. They helped with archival research, scanned numerous images and contributed to various chapters. The Sherman Fairchild Foundation, the Dean of Faculty's Office and the History Department at Colby College funded their efforts and this project. Pat Burdick and Erin Rhodes of Special Collections at Miller Library located newspaper microfilms and old books. Quili Wang and Erfan Azad of Colby's Language Resource Center assisted with image scanning and created DVDs of old videos. Lauren Lessing of the Colby Art Museum offered advice on image preparation. Manny Gimond patiently designed maps.

Beyond the local area, Maine Historical Society staff, especially John Mayer, Dani Fazio and Sofia Yalouris, located rarely seen objects, photos and archival material. Amy Bell Segal of Terrence J. DeWan & Associates shared her vision for the future of Fort Halifax Park.

A final note of thanks goes to Katie Orlando, editor at The History Press, whose patient attention has made this project possible and enjoyable.

I am grateful for all those who helped with this project and those who continue the difficult work of maintaining the blockhouse and preserving its history.

Introduction
Winslow's Historic Outpost

It is the symbol of Winslow: the wooden blockhouse that sits near the entrance to a public park just off the main thoroughfare. At a glance, the square, two-story structure made of hewn timbers with a hipped roof, perched along the Sebasticook River near its confluence with the Kennebec, does not seem like much. Few people realize that the blockhouse they see today—and can rarely peek inside—is the oldest blockhouse in the United States and a National Historic Landmark. Few realize that it was only a small fraction of a large colonial fort. Fort Halifax, built when Maine was still part of Massachusetts, once dominated the Maine wilderness. Few people are aware of the subsequent story of the lone blockhouse and the land on which it stands. Few people know of Fort Halifax's battle against neglect, nature and economic change. Far more than initially meets the eye, Fort Halifax has been the central and defining feature of the town of Winslow since its construction in 1754.

A complete history of Fort Halifax, showcasing the fort's various lives and the meaning of these changes, is long overdue. Previously, the most detailed publication on Fort Halifax was a short booklet, *The History of Fort Halifax*, by Carleton E. Fisher. Though helpful, the book focuses exclusively on the construction of the fort, its manpower and its weaponry during the French and Indian War of 1754–63. Other books of local and regional interest have mentioned Fort Halifax only in passing.

Additionally, articles related to Fort Halifax have frequently appeared in the leading newspaper in central Maine, the *Morning Sentinel*, and its predecessors for over 150 years. Crucial information is available in newspaper clippings and microfilm reels, but only for those who want to do some substantial digging. In addition, seldom-used personal accounts, state and local government reports, town council minutes, archaeological investigations and civic organizations' records shine light on this place's long and significant history and tell a story that needs to be told. Seldom seen historical portraits, photographs and modern images from the private collections of local townspeople, historical societies and local libraries are interspersed through the text.

Using these sources, this book pieces together the fort's complex story. It traces the story of Fort Halifax from beginning to end, from prehistory to the present. In particular, it analyzes the cares and concerns of the people who have inhabited and visited this spot. Fort Halifax and Winslow, Maine, have been inseparably linked. From an outpost built on an ancient Indian fishing village, to a small colonial settlement, to a farming community, to an industrial center, to a bedroom community redefining itself in the twenty-first century, Winslow and its people have changed and transformed. The fort and its remnants have evolved with each historical shift, continually serving as a reflection of the conditions, attitudes and economic climate of Winslow.

Native Americans inhabited the land on which the fort resides far before its construction. However, a lack of written and preserved history has caused historians to rely on a few personal accounts of explorers and archaeological evidence to understand more about the people and the large Abenaki village that existed here. Geography appears to be the key to understanding the significance of this spot. The meeting place of the Kennebec and Sebasticook Rivers provided the connection point between a vast network of trading and tribal alliances, making it the logical area of thousands of years of Native American habitation.

The geographic significance of this point also placed it at the center of colonial expansion and defense. Starting in the seventeenth century, the British based in the Plymouth Colony of Massachusetts and the French based in Quebec both aimed at increasing their colonial footholds. Maine, part of Massachusetts until 1820 and centered between the two colonial empires, became the battleground. A mixture of political and economic factors caused the British to build Fort Halifax in 1754. The Seven Years' War, or French and Indian War, provided the impetus for the construction of a military outpost. Furthermore, the lobbying of powerful investors and land speculators in Massachusetts called for a fort to encourage white settlement in the Kennebec River Valley.

While militarily quiet—except for several skirmishes with Native Americans—Fort Halifax brought settlement to the area and displaced native peoples, leading to the establishment of Winslow in 1771. Through this period, the town and the fort began a deep and lasting relationship. Both grew and existed through a mutual dependence, fostering a connection that has continued to the present.

During the Revolution, Benedict Arnold relied on Fort Halifax as an encampment and supply stop, which he used to attack Quebec in 1775. It also served Penobscot Indians displaced by the British occupation of the Penobscot River. During and since Arnold's visit, Fort Halifax was used as a dance hall, tavern and place for town meetings and worship before it was torn down in the late 1790s. By 1800, only one lone blockhouse remained.

Through the following century, the fort transitioned from an outpost on the colonial frontier to the center of growing settlement and community. Historians Timothy Otis Paine and William Goold and numerous journalists documented the fort's enduring and valuable presence. Yet its existence was never a given. Despite historic preservation efforts in the 1870s, the blockhouse fell into disrepair. Souvenir hunters regularly plundered it. Meanwhile, industrialization drastically changed the social and economic structure of Winslow and the Kennebec River Valley. Increasingly, the fort became associated with an antiquated and poorly remembered past, contributing to neglect that led to its slow deterioration.

A powerful sense of historical nostalgia overtook the economic and industrial transformations of the late nineteenth and early twentieth centuries. From 1913 to 1966, restoration efforts led by a local chapter of the Daughters of the Revolution preserved the blockhouse and ensured its continued existence. Bicentennials and various memorials helped to keep the fort in the collective consciousness of the town of Winslow. A massive community effort began in 1970, feeding off this intense historical interest. In a process that took more than a decade to realize, Winslow's dedicated citizens converted the land where the fort once stood into a public park, revitalizing it as a symbol at the center of the town.

Fort Halifax's blockhouse survived general neglect, a railroad fire and several major floods. The greatest force it ever faced occurred in the spring of 1987, when a massive flood swept it downriver. Testifying to their commitment to this historic symbol, the residents and civic organizations of Winslow came to the rescue. With state assistance, they gathered the blockhouse's broken pieces. After several archaeological digs, Stan Mathieu beautifully restored the blockhouse and the surrounding park. Much fanfare followed. Since the reconstruction of the blockhouse in 1988, Winslow residents have engaged in much debate over how the Fort Halifax blockhouse and park should fit into the town's future, and the story of Fort Halifax continues to be written. The residents' dedication to Fort Halifax continues with more recent efforts to improve the site.

Over the years, Fort Halifax has proven its ability to change with the times. Like Winslow, its meanings, interpretations and identity have been reshaped and remolded. The fort's blockhouse has served as everything from a cow pen to a site for romanticist musings to a backdrop for anti-communist speeches in the 1950s. Today, it hosts weddings, picnics, concerts, kayakers and fishermen. It also hosts central Maine's largest gathering, the annual Winslow Family Fourth of July Celebration, attended by tens of thousands of people.

Fort Halifax is more than just a lonely blockhouse. It is the symbol of a town and its people. Fort Halifax has withstood the battle waged by time, nature and civilization. And in the pages of this book, its story comes to life in the hopes that future generations will continue to enjoy its rich and multilayered story.

Chapter 1

Indians and Pilgrims: Fort Point before 1754

For five thousand years, Native Americans have inhabited the Kennebec River Valley. Archaeologists have found burials and artifacts older than the pyramids of Egypt, including American Indian burial sites with the red powder from iron ochre. Some call these Indians the Red Paint People. Archaeological evidence suggests that 3,200 years ago, the peninsula called "Fort Point" at the confluence of the Sebasticook and the Kennebec Rivers, just south of Taconnet (or Ticonic today) Falls, was the "seasonal home of as many as 500 Indians who camped there to spear migrating sturgeon," according to archaeologist Art Speiss of the Maine Historic Preservation Commission. Native peoples fished and lived along the two rivers for thousands of years at a location of geographical and economic significance.[1]

Seventeenth-century French explorers and settlers used the term *Abenaquois*—or "People of the Dawnland"—to refer to the Indians living in northern New England west of the Penobscot River. The English called those native peoples "Abenakis." They are one tribe of what became the Wabanaki Confederacy. Five thousand Abenakis, the Kennebec Indians, lived in four main villages in the Kennebec River Valley.[2] By the early 1600s, they lived at present-day Richmond, at the head of the tide at Cushnoc (today Augusta) and between the mouth of the Sebasticook and Taconnet Falls in present-day Winslow. The Norridgewocks lived at Old Point in the present town of Madison. Thousands of other Indians lived elsewhere along the rivers, lakes and coastal regions of Maine.[3]

Like the Indians who came before them, these tribes knew well the strategic importance of the Taconnet Falls region. *Taconnet* derives from the Abenaki word meaning "a place to cross." Indians frequently crossed the Kennebec River at the falls, between what are now Waterville and Winslow. The meeting of the two rivers represented the intersection of two major travel routes.[4] Indians from Canada, as well as Kennebec Indians traveling to and from Norridgewock, passed that way. For centuries, Penobscot Indians journeyed from their homelands along the Penobscot River more than fifty miles northeast. Once they reached the Sebasticook, they canoed downstream to Taconnet and then descended the Kennebec to trade, fight and make peace. North of Taconnet Falls, the Kennebec had numerous rapids and portages; Taconnet divided easy travel to the south and not-so-easy travel to the north. Taconnet occupied an important place in the geography of the region.[5] Given this importance, it is no surprise the Indians had a settlement here. Around the turn of the seventeenth century, according to Richard Hakluyt, a Kennebec Indian village called Ketangheanycke stood on the east bank of the Kennebec, in between the mouth of the Sebasticook to the south and Taconnet Falls to the north. The second-largest Indian village in Maine in the early 1600s, it had ninety wigwams and roughly 330 warriors. Its population exceeded one thousand.[6]

By the early 1600s, the English and the French were attempting to establish permanent footholds in North America. Maine's native peoples faced new challenges. As they competed for allies and resources, they succumbed to devastating epidemic diseases. In the midst of this chaos, the first traders arrived on the Kennebec. In 1624, the Plymouth Colony began its fur trade with the Native Americans along the Kennebec River. In 1625, Governor William Bradford sent Edward Winslow up the Kennebec River. Winslow set up a trading post at present-day Augusta and traded corn with the Kennebec Indians in exchange for beaver skins and other furs.[7] Intrigued, Bradford and his associates secured land on the Kennebec from the Plymouth Council, the joint stock company located in England that had been granted the land from the Crown. The Plymouth Council soon folded. The Pilgrims now controlled a large tract on the Kennebec. Neither their post at modern Augusta nor their post at present-day Castine proved profitable.[8]

The French, headquartered in Quebec City, lacked the manpower and the resources to establish themselves in North America. But they did their best to send priests, to trade with the Indians and to undermine English interests. A French Jesuit, Father Gabriel Druilletes, ministered to native

Edward Winslow, by School of Robert Walker, 1651. *Pilgrim Hall Museum.*

peoples between what are now Augusta and Norridgewock and briefly ran a mission near modern-day Augusta in the late 1640s.[9]

Indians expanded their trade opportunities in the region. In 1649, a Kennebec sachem, Canibas (or Kenebis) deeded lands to Massachusetts trader Christopher Lawson, an agent of the trading firm owned by Thomas Clark and Thomas Lake of Boston. He set up a trading post on the south shore of the Sebasticook, where it enters the Kennebec River. He traded cloth and kettles for furs from his blockhouse before transferring ownership to Clark and Lake in 1653. By 1654, Richard Hammond established a second trading post at Taconnet, on the north side of the river and near the Indian village, one of three he founded on the Kennebec.[10]

Soon the native inhabitants began to realize—and to demand—the fair value of their beaver skins. The Pilgrims lost interest in the area as profit margins decreased. In 1661, Plymouth Colony sold its lands on the Kennebec to four men known as the "Kennebec Proprietors," also referred to as the Plymouth Company.[11] They and their heirs held the land for decades but did little with it.

In 1675, war erupted in southern New England between Wampanoags under King Philip (Metacom) and English colonists. Kennebec Indians had concerns of their own: the rapid pace of English settlement and access to trade goods. The English feared that the Indians of present-day Maine would ally themselves with Philip or the French or would supply weapons to Indian enemies of the colonies. English authorities coerced several tribal leaders to lay down their arms. Soon after, Captain Sylvanus Davis from Clark and Lake's post at Arrowsic sent a messenger to Taconnet to remove the guns that were in the trading house there. The messenger carried a promise to the Indians that if they came to Arrowsic, they would get their supplies. But instead, he instructed them that "if they did not go down and give up their arms the English would come up and kill them." From the village in Taconnet, the Indians reached out to the Massachusetts officials. The Indians needed guns and ammunition for hunting. The English felt that if they sold them these, they were providing for their own destruction. Davis and an English agent named Abraham Shurte came to Taconnet for a diplomatic visit. The Taconnets declared their peaceful intentions, but key issues remained unresolved.[12]

Tensions came to a head when the trader Richard Hammond plied the Indians with rum, got them drunk and stole their furs. In revenge, Kennebecs reached Hammond's post at Woolwich on August 13, 1676. They burned it and killed him and two others. The next day, Kennebecs attacked Clark and Lake's trading post at Arrowsic and destroyed it. They killed Clark and Davis and wounded several others. The Indians returned to Taconnet with perhaps fifty prisoners, including Hammond's wife, Elizabeth. Not until April 1678 did various Kennebec leaders sign a treaty and release the prisoners. At least 260 white settlers of Maine had been killed. The toll for the Native Americans was far greater.[13]

From 1688 to 1697, another imperial war raged in North America, King William's War. In 1691, Kennebec Indians attacked English settlements far to the south. Taconnet, as a center for communication and transportation, served as an entrepôt for English prisoners. The government at Boston sent veteran Indian fighter Benjamin Church to the Kennebec to kill Indians on sight. In 1692, Church defeated an army of Indians on the lower Kennebec and then ascended the river to Taconnet. White men claimed that the Indians torched the fortified village on Fort Point, then fled. Indians claimed that white men burned and looted the place. Either way, Indians never permanently returned to the site. Many Kennebec Indians scattered to Norridgewock Village and others to Abenaki villages in Quebec.[14]

French leaders in Quebec refounded the French mission on the Kennebec in 1693 and centered it among the Norridgewocks. Massachusetts authorities viewed the Jesuit there, Father Sebastien Rasle, with suspicion. Indeed, for several decades, he had provided religious instruction, mediated community conflict and compiled an Abenaki dictionary. He also incited Abenakis to go on the warpath against the English. For years, Abenakis raided the Maine coast, destroying settlements and taking captives. After two unsuccessful expeditions up the Kennebec in 1721 and 1722, Massachusetts troops returned in 1724. Leaving their boats and forty men at Taconnet, the rest marched to Norridgewock. They attacked Rasle's mission church, killing him and dozens of others. By 1748, few Abenakis remained on the Kennebec. English officials and colonial records referred to these inhabitants simply as "Norridgewocks." In reality, some of the Kennebec Indians lived in that village. Most of them, after years of population decline due to disease and war, migrated to villages on the outskirts of Quebec City, such as St. Francis, Wolinak, Odanak and Becancour.[15]

By 1749, the French had pushed closer to British claims in North America. French and British interests were clashing yet again. Nine of the heirs of the original Kennebec Proprietors of 1661 devised a scheme to open the Kennebec Valley for settlement. They petitioned Governor William Shirley to build a fort. Indian warfare and French encroachment threatened the interests of Massachusetts and the proprietors. The number of white settlers was few and far between, and most of them could not be called permanent. "Most of them were seasonal trappers, unmarried men, or men who for the trapping season, left their wives and families in a more settled region."[16] A stronger British presence in the region would provide security and promote permanent white settlement. And Massachusetts had already faced thirty-five years of warfare with French and Indian enemies, as well as devastating raids.[17] In 1753, the Kennebec Proprietors again petitioned Governor Shirley to build a fort at Taconnet. As another period of warfare loomed, Massachusetts investors and government officials—sometimes one and the same—eyed the confluence of the Kennebec and Sebasticook Rivers. Little did they know, the fort they would build would forever shape the identity of a community.

Chapter 2

General Winslow Builds Fort Halifax, 1754

On June 22, 1754, nearly three weeks after he had left his hometown of Concord, Massachusetts, John Barber, the clerk in Captain Eleazer Melvin's Massachusetts militia company, embarked from Cambridge on the sloop *Success*. Barber and five hundred men—soon joined by another three hundred—sailed north. Their final destination was the former Abenaki village at Taconnet Falls. A day after departing, Barber wrote, the ships "[c]ame on the Most Violent Storm that Ever Was Known." The storm gained in strength, and the "[m]en almost all of them [were] Sea Sick," Barber added. "It tore away our Gibb Saile Which Put our Men into a Great Surprise." They sailed into Casco Bay on June 26. The Kennebec awaited; the adventure had just begun.[18]

The expedition, first imagined in the petitions of the Kennebec Proprietors in 1749 and 1753, became a reality as imperial tensions flared and the economic benefits became clearer. By May 1754, preparations were underway for a military expedition to investigate French activities at the head of the Kennebec, the construction of a fort at Taconnet Falls, a fortified storehouse the government would call the Storehouse at Cushnoc and the Kennebec Proprietors would call "Fort Western" and the first carriage road north of Cushnoc, present-day Augusta.[19]

In February 1754, Governor Shirley received reports that the French in Canada were building a fort at the portage between the Kennebec and Chaudière Rivers at the Great Carrying Place. A large party of Indians appeared at Fort Richmond, "using threatening language, which were suspected to be spies from Canada." French priests in Maine were allegedly stirring up Indian discontent. Massachusetts was on the verge of a sixth Indian war since 1675. The assemblymen declared their determination to block any French advance. A fort just below Taconnet Falls, Governor Shirley wrote, would sever communication among Maine Indian tribes. Though the Indians could cross between the Kennebec and Sebasticook in present-day Clinton, about ten miles above Taconnet, they would have to go three or four miles through the woods and would be vulnerable to ambush. A fort would offer "a strong curb" against French and Indian military campaigns. In a speech to both houses of the legislature on March 28, 1754, Governor Shirley urged lawmakers to take "[v]igorous Measures against the French."[20]

On April 2, the House ordered that an investigative military expedition take place. Governor Shirley sent Captain James Bane of Fort Frederick at Pemaquid Point and Bane's brother Jonathan to look for signs of French or Indian activities at the Great Carrying Place. He also ordered them to scout the land between Cushnoc and Taconnet Falls for timber availability. Shirley also sent Captains John North and Samuel Goodwin, Kennebec Proprietors living at Frankfort—present-day Dresden—to "[s]urvey for the Proprietors and Inhabitants" and view timber availability.[21]

Between April 3 and April 17, the Massachusetts legislature, the governor and the Kennebec Proprietors colluded on a mutually beneficial scheme. The province would build a fort at Taconnet. Massachusetts assemblymen agreed to employ five hundred men to build the fort and approved £5,300 to cover expenses.[22] A fort, however, required a storehouse and foothold at the head of the tide to hold supplies. At the same time, the Kennebec Proprietors agreed to construct a fortified storehouse at Cushnoc—a supply depot—for the larger fort eighteen miles north at Taconnet. Massachusetts offered cannons and troops to protect the workmen and supplies during the construction process. Governor Shirley also planned to build a road between the two new forts, to facilitate the transportation of supplies and to "greatly incourage [*sic*] Settlements upon it."[23]

To be sure, this was a boon for the Kennebec Proprietors. No inhabitants but seasonal trappers and frontiersmen lived north of Cushnoc. Settlement would increase by providing security and deterring Indian attacks and by offering contracts for soldiers' provisions. Investors would make money. There is further evidence of the collusion between Massachusetts and the Plymouth Company. The governor's daughter married a large shareholder in the Plymouth Company on April 14. And before the end of the year, another proprietor had conveyed shares to Governor Shirley. Many believe that the fort was a scheme of the Plymouth Company to further settlement and add to the value of its lands.[24]

On May 7, the Plymouth Company hired Boston builder Gershom Flagg to build the storehouse at Cushnoc. A half-share owner in the company, Flagg supervised and hired workers for the Taconnet Fort. Later, he would design Pownalborough Courthouse in what is today Dresden, Maine, and would renovate King's Chapel and John Hancock's mansion in Boston.[25]

In June, while Barber and other militiamen gathered at Castle William, the legislators voted another three hundred officers and men to join the five hundred already allotted. Each enlisted man provided his own arms in exchange for a one shilling, six pence bounty.[26]

Governor Shirley appointed Major General John Winslow to lead the troops and construction workers. Born in Marshfield, Massachusetts, he was the great-grandson of Edward Winslow, a *Mayflower* passenger and trader. A great-uncle, John Winslow, had made the trading voyage up the Kennebec 130 years earlier and helped set up the Pilgrim trading post at Cushnoc. In 1661, John Winslow was one of the four men who bought the Plymouth patent. The Winslow family still owned a large share in the Plymouth Company. Shirley thought highly of Major General Winslow. He "hath the best reputation, as a military man, of any officer in this province, and his character in every respect stands high with the government and people," the governor wrote, "and he is particularly well esteemed by the soldiery." A year later, Winslow would undertake a different mission. In 1755, he would oversee the forced deportation of Acadians, the French-speaking farmers and fishermen in Nova Scotia who had refused to pledge allegiance to the British Empire.[27]

General John Winslow, by Joseph Blackburn. *Pilgrim Hall Museum.*

When John Barber and the first of the troops under Major General Winslow sailed into Casco Bay, they camped on an island just east of present-day South Portland. Today, this is Cushing Island. Two days later, Governor Shirley arrived on the sloop of war *Massachusetts*. He invited Norridgewock and Penobscot Indians to meet with him. But the conference, he admitted, was a mere formality. He "had determin'd to have the march made…and to have Forts erected…whether they gave their Consent or not." Norridgewock Indian representatives at first refused to sign anything. Plied with liquor, they relented on July 2. Penobscot Indians hesitated to meet with the governor, but the troops were already in motion. On July 4, Winslow and a fleet of "two Gundeloes, Nine Whale Boats, and 40 Battoes" sailed from Casco Bay up the Kennebec River. On July 5, the Penobscots met with the governor. The parties formally signed a treaty the following day.[28]

Governor Shirley and the Massachusetts Council stayed in Falmouth, where they ran the Massachusetts government and coordinated the expedition.[29] The soldiers sailed up the Kennebec. They paused for a few days at Fort Richmond, a Massachusetts post on the west side of the river opposite the upper end of Swan Island. Then they proceeded upriver with three hundred tons of hand-hewn timber for Cushnoc. On about July 12, they reached their destination. Gershom Flagg started construction. Colonel Jedediah Preble and Captain Eleazer Melvin went upriver in whaleboats with forty-two men to pinpoint the location for the new fort at Taconnet.[30]

On July 25, Major General Winslow and ten companies of troops followed. The rocky shoals between Cushnoc and Taconnet made navigation treacherous. Not only were there six rips to navigate, but also the water was shallower than expected. Soldiers pushed their boats over rocky and sandy areas and fought the current.[31] On July 27 at Taconnet, Winslow held a council with his captains and agreed to build the fort "[w]here the Plymouth Company had Built a fort above one hundred years Since (42) Paces Longe." Was Winslow mistaken? Or had there been a third trading post in the seventeenth century? He drafted a plan, and work commenced under the management of Isaac Ilsley and Gershom Flagg. With eighteen carpenters, several skilled craftsmen and masons, apprentices and the work of soldiers, construction proceeded quickly.[32] The fort's construction crew included eighteen-year-old Enoch Poor.[33] Poor would become a brigadier general in the Revolutionary War and distinguish himself at Saratoga, in the Battle of Monmouth and in the Sullivan Expedition against the Iroquois Indians.

Meanwhile, Governor Shirley ordered 500 men to march north along the Kennebec to look for French settlements between Taconnet Falls and

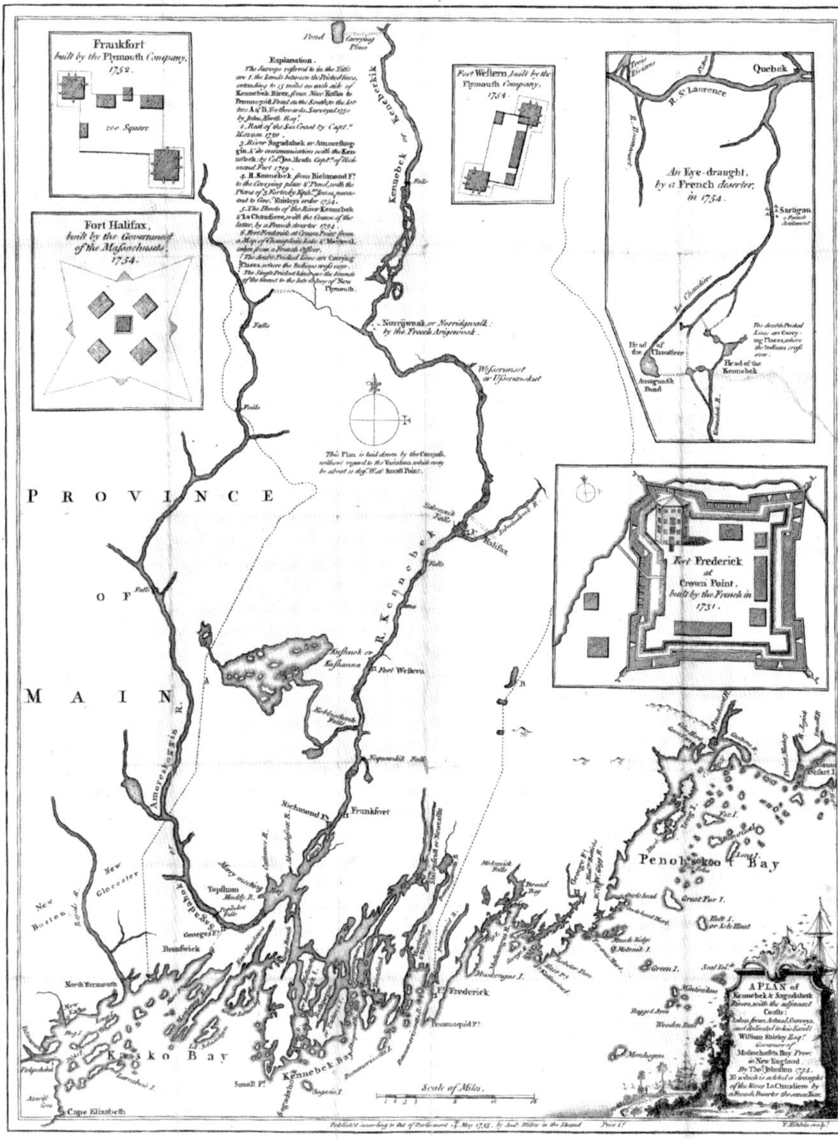

"A Plan of Kennebek & Sagadahok Rivers," by Thomas Johnston, 1754. *Maine Historical Society.*

the Chaudière River in Quebec. Winslow left Taconnet on August 8 with 506 men. Surveyors made measurements and drew maps. Winslow got sick two days later and turned back, leaving his highest-ranking officer, Colonel Jedediah Preble of Falmouth, in command. Preble's men proceeded

Old Fort Western, 2013. *Author photo.*

beyond Skowhegan and up Norridgewock Falls. They journeyed beyond the Sandy River and past Caratunk to the west fork of the Kennebec. On August 18, they reached the Great Carrying Place, the portage between the Kennebec and Dead Rivers. When they got to the first pond, they turned back. On August 21, the troops paused in Norridgewock again. Thirty-five Indians met with them and once again confirmed peace. The soldiers had found no French fort and no French soldiers. They saw only a few Indians along the way outside Norridgewock, and those Indians were friendly or fled in fear after seeing such a large force so far advanced into the wilderness. The expedition returned to Taconnet on August 23, where construction continued.[34] Most of the soldiers had returned to Falmouth by August 29. But 120 soldiers remained at Taconnet. Another 20 men garrisoned Fort Western. Carpenters and laborers continued their efforts until mid-November.[35]

On August 30, the governor left Falmouth to visit the forts. He visited Fort Western and spent the night on board the *Massachusetts*. The next day, Shirley journeyed by whaleboat to the new fort. Two hundred of Winslow's soldiers guarded him by marching along the shore. The governor led a ceremony at the fort, probably on September 1. He laid a cornerstone in the central blockhouse built by Winslow—which eventually became the north flanker in

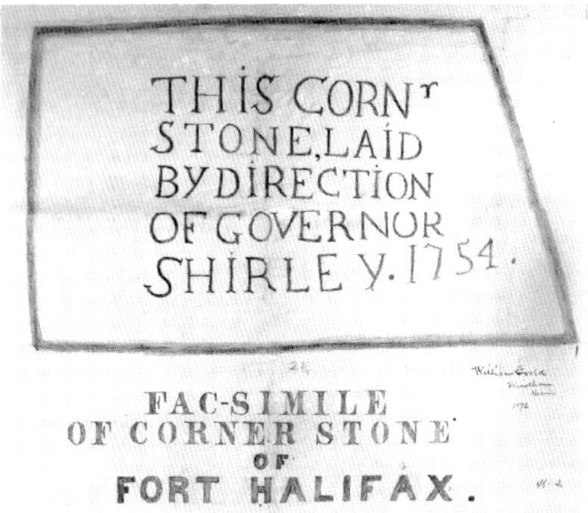

Sketch of the Fort Halifax cornerstone, by William Goold, 1876. *Maine Historical Society.*

the fortress when completed. Shirley also laid a memorial stone at the fort, which he named Fort Halifax.[36]

In recent years, the locations of the cornerstone and memorial stone have attracted some interest. Both seem to have vanished. In the 1820s, William Freeman reportedly gave the cornerstone to Asa Redington Jr. In 1845, Redington, a circuit court judge whose father once owned property near the fort, reportedly delivered the cornerstone, or a copy of it, to the Maine Statehouse. In 1972, historian Carleton Fisher attempted to find the cornerstone, but no one at the Maine State Museum or other state offices knew anything about it. A disappointed Fisher reported that "[h]earsay evidence was repeated that some years ago when the state house lawn was being landscaped it may have been thrown in a hole for fill." According to another source dated 1908, "this valuable relic was," in fact, "removed from the State House at the time of one of its recent renovations, and...was deposited in the geological cabinets of Colby College at Waterville." In 2013, a search of the Geology Department and Miller Library's Special Collections turned up no such "relic." The memorial stone also seems to have disappeared. Dr. Isaac Winslow, son of Major General Winslow, apparently removed it and transported it to the family's estate in Marshfield, Massachusetts, after his father's death in 1771. By 1852, the Winslow family property had changed hands several times. But it was "in his front door yard." No mention of it appears after that in the historical record, and when contacted in 2013, the staff at the Dr. Isaac Winslow House had no knowledge of its whereabouts.[37]

With the soldiers drawn up under arms, the *Boston News-Letter* reported, the governor "drank success to Fort Halifax; which was seconded by a general Discharge of the Cannon there." The Earl of Halifax was a logical namesake for the fort on the Kennebec and Sebasticook. Born in 1716 as George Montagu, he earned a reputation as an "extremely brilliant" scholar at Eton College and Trinity College, Cambridge. He became the Second

George Montagu Dunk, Second Earl of Halifax, K.G., by Sir Joshua Reynolds, 1764. *Art Gallery of Nova Scotia.*

Earl of Halifax upon his father's death in 1739. Two years later, Halifax acquired a small fortune when he married a sixteen-year-old. He took her surname and soon inherited her father's estate. After working for the royal family and holding several government posts, he became president of the Board of Trade in 1748. He expanded its oversight of colonial economic and political affairs. He also worked tirelessly to defend the frontiers of British America from the French and their Indian allies. A year later, he helped to found the British outpost at Halifax, later the capital of Nova Scotia. Lord Halifax spent extravagantly and drank heavily. He also devoted much of his attention to his mistress, for whom he later built a mansion.[38]

Leaving behind the workers, the 120 men at Fort Halifax and another 20 soldiers at Fort Western, Shirley and the remainder of the troops sailed for Falmouth and then to Boston.[39] The ten-week expedition was complete at a cost of 13,782 pounds, 4 shillings, 3 pence. In just eight weeks of labor, Winslow's soldiers had journeyed to the carrying place. Workers had built the storehouse of Fort Western. Soldiers, carpenters and craftsmen had built Fort Halifax. Eighteen miles of cleared roads connected the two forts.[40]

Though they had accomplished much, the builders of Fort Halifax had endured injury, illness and numerous hardships. Several men were hurt. Many, like Second Lieutenant Thomas Lawrence, a native of Groton, Massachusetts, successfully petitioned the General Court for disability compensation. Five weeks after he returned to Boston, Lawrence still needed medical care. While "laying down one of the plank, which was too heavy for me, it gave me a sudden Rinch," he added, "which I often feel the effects of, and shall, as long as I live." To add insult to injury, he wrote, "soon after [I] was taken with a slow fever." It still lingered weeks later when he submitted his petition on October 30, 1754. He needed, but could not afford, a wheelchair. The General Court awarded him eleven pounds, ten shillings, seven pence. It showed similar compassion for other soldiers.[41]

When Major General Winslow returned home, the fort was not nearly complete. After eighty-two days of labor, a two-story blockhouse overlooked the Kennebec and provided a view upriver. The lower story was twenty feet square and the upper story, twenty-seven feet square. It had four one-story barracks, each twenty feet square. The barracks were placed opposite the corners of the blockhouse. Winslow intended for a high fence—a palisade—to enclose the complex. The palisade was to surround the fort in the shape of a four-pointed star. The center of each side was to contain an elevated platform from which to fire. A gate through the picket was to sit on the west. But the pickets for the palisade were not yet in place. A second, smaller blockhouse, called a redoubt, stood atop the high ground to the northeast of the main fortification. Winslow planned to fence it in, too. Troops had brought cannons for the two blockhouses. But much work remained to be done. Though timbers and bricks were available, several

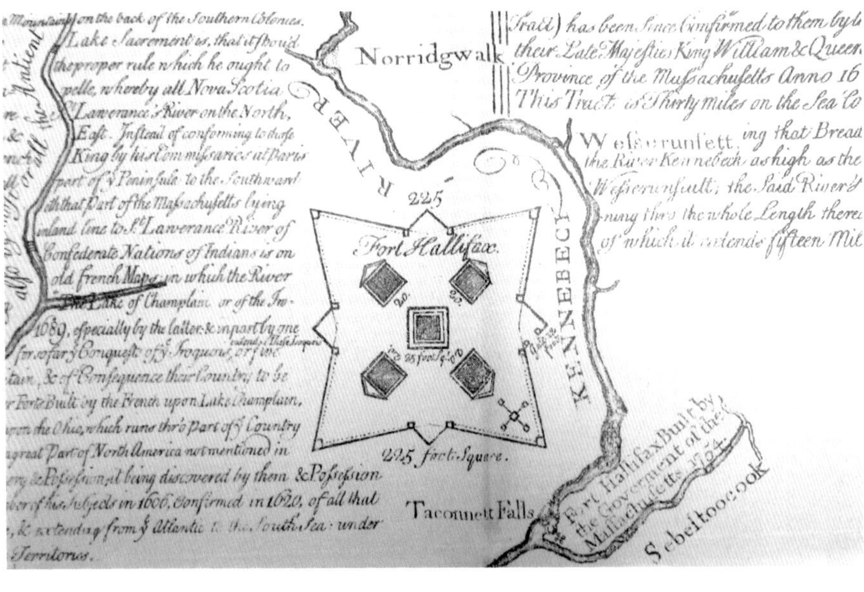

Detail of "A Plan of Kennebek & Sagadahok Rivers," by Thomas Johnston, 1754. *From a 1912 reprint by the Massachusetts Historical Society.*

structures intended to be built had not yet been started: officers' quarters, a guardhouse and an armorer's shop. A well had not yet been dug. When Winslow left, Fort Halifax was not yet half built.[42]

In its current state, how defensible was Fort Halifax? Because the French would not transport cannons and mortars by land, Fort Halifax seemed safe from an artillery assault. But Indians hiding in the woods posed a different threat altogether. On October 30, 1754, a detachment of ten men and a team of oxen cut and hauled firewood. Eight Indians lay in ambush. "As they were coming back the Indians fired upon them," Colonel Israel Williams wrote, "and killed one man and scalp'd him." Thomas Newman of Lynn, Massachusetts, fell dead. Indians captured four other men. They chased a sixth man "and threw their Hatchets after him," an express from the fort reported. But the wounded man retreated into Fort Halifax.[43] The governor urged the House of Representatives to take action. The House proposed stopping the shipment of gifts to the Indians. It voted to send reinforcements to Fort Halifax. Only nineteen men appeared—and not until February. The House also authorized Captain William Lithgow of Fort Richmond to impress men into service if enlistment did not provide enough soldiers.[44]

Adding to the garrison's woes, bread, rum, molasses and other items ran low. On November 12, 1754, the House of Representatives had passed an order directing the commissary general to provide one hundred pairs of snowshoes and moccasins for the garrison. But fearing French privateers, Governor Shirley stopped those goods, and the shipment to the several Maine forts was delayed for twenty-six days. As winter set in, the ailing and undersupplied soldiers at Fort Halifax feared further attacks from Indians. Indians hoped to drive out what they perceived as a bold attempt by Europeans to encroach on tribal lands.[45]

Chapter 3

Renovating and Manning Fort Halifax, 1755–1770

Born in Ireland, William Lithgow came to Boston with his Irish mother, Janet; his Scottish father, Robert; and two older sisters when he was an infant. The family moved to present-day Maine, and his father worked as a surveyor. They were among the first inhabitants of the town of Topsham. During Massachusetts's war with the Abenaki Indians from 1721 to 1725, Robert Lithgow joined the Massachusetts colonial troops, and the family moved to the fort in present-day Brunswick. In 1734, after training as a gunsmith, William followed in his father's footsteps and joined the military. He absorbed a wealth of experience by living and serving in frontier outposts. He served as "armourer" at Fort St. George, located in present-day Thomaston. In 1746, he wooed and married Sarah Noble of Georgetown. Sarah was ten years his junior and the daughter of a military man. A few promotions later, in 1748, Lithgow assumed command of Fort Richmond on the Kennebec. In a portrait painted in the 1760s, he appears confident and comfortable. As the Church of England's missionary on the Kennebec, Reverend Jacob Bailey wrote, Lithgow "was a fair dealer, a lover of peace, had a proper command of his temper, was easy, sociable, and good-humoured." Bailey also lamented that Lithgow was not religiously inclined. Nonetheless, his years in the military and his good social skills made him ideally suited for the rigors of frontier garrison life. He also apparently spoke dialects of the Eastern Abenaki language.[46]

Lithgow seemed a logical choice to command and improve Fort Halifax. But he was not Governor Shirley's first choice. In December 1754, a committee from the House of Representatives recommended that the

William Lithgow, by Joseph Badger, circa 1760. *Colby College Museum of Art, Gift of Mr. and Mrs. Ellerton Jetté, 1982.005.*

governor appoint some qualified person to take charge of Fort Halifax. Shirley tapped Colonel Jedediah Preble—who led the march to the Great Carrying Place that August. Preble apparently declined. Lithgow, then commander of Richmond Fort, had come to Fort Halifax in October 1754 to direct some work there. On January 3, the governor had ordered Lithgow, if Preble declined, to "make Provision for strengthening the Fotresses" and to "proceed to the Compleating & finishing of the sd Work accord to Order without delay." Shirley also ordered Lithgow to employ the soldiers "in Scouting for Discovery of the Enemy" and "for obtaining a better Knowledge of the Country." Captain Lithgow assumed command of a post he would hold for over a decade.[47]

As 1755 began, Captain Lithgow faced some significant obstacles. Overcrowding, poor supplies and illness threatened the lives of the troops.

Continual marches, wet conditions and capsizing boats had rendered blankets, knapsacks and bandoliers (the shoulder belt used to hold ammunition) "unserviceable."[48]

Difficult conditions also weakened the soldiers. On January 4, Captain Lithgow sized up the state of his garrison. Fewer than half of the men were able to cut and split the firewood they so desperately needed to warm the drafty barracks. Bread, rum, molasses and other provisions ran low. Morale was slipping. "A grate many" were sick and dying. Herbal remedies ran low, and "our Docter has left us," Lithgow reported. The governor sent physician Dr. John Calef of Ipswich, Massachusetts, to the fort. Calef arrived in early February and continued until April 1. Muster rolls show that five men died during the winter of 1754–55, two officers and three "Centinells." Additionally, Lithgow wrote, "the Snow is so Deep, it is 3 foot at this Place," and they had no snowshoes.[49]

The one hundred pairs each of snowshoes and moccasins, and the warm bedding and blankets that Lithgow expected, had not arrived before the end of 1754. On January 2, the assembly authorized the commissary to send supplies up to the fort. A sloop laden with these supplies and with other provisions reached Arrowsic on the lower Kennebec. Captain Lithgow and another soldier were already en route to meet the supplies. The journey there was perilous. The ice was weak and thin—"[s]o weak that we Broak throw Sundery Times," he wrote. A storm detained them at Fort Western. They reached Richmond Fort on January 8 and arrived at Arrowsic a day or two later. Snow drifted ten to fifteen feet high, making the roads impassable on the return trip, but the chill froze the river. Over a three-week period, Lithgow and more than five dozen men hauled two hundred barrels of supplies up the icy Kennebec on hand sleds. Militia captains David Dunning of Brunswick and Adam Hunter of Topsham (Lithgow's brother-in-law) and nineteen of their men joined Lithgow and forty men from Fort Halifax and Fort Western.[50] The governor sent additional provisions and clothing shortly after.[51]

The problems with supplies and with the soldiers' health, discipline and morale had left Lithgow without "one Days Rest In body or mind." These problems hindered his ability to maintain order. Many of the fort's soldiers were drafted into service from the poorest ranks. Lithgow considered them ill-suited for frontier duty. He called them "Cretures that Resembels men In nothing but ye Humain Shape." He wished he had "Dissmised Som worthless Fellows," who did little more than eat and sleep, "for thay will never Do any Service here or any whers else." But he was short on manpower, too, so he kept them on the muster rolls.[52]

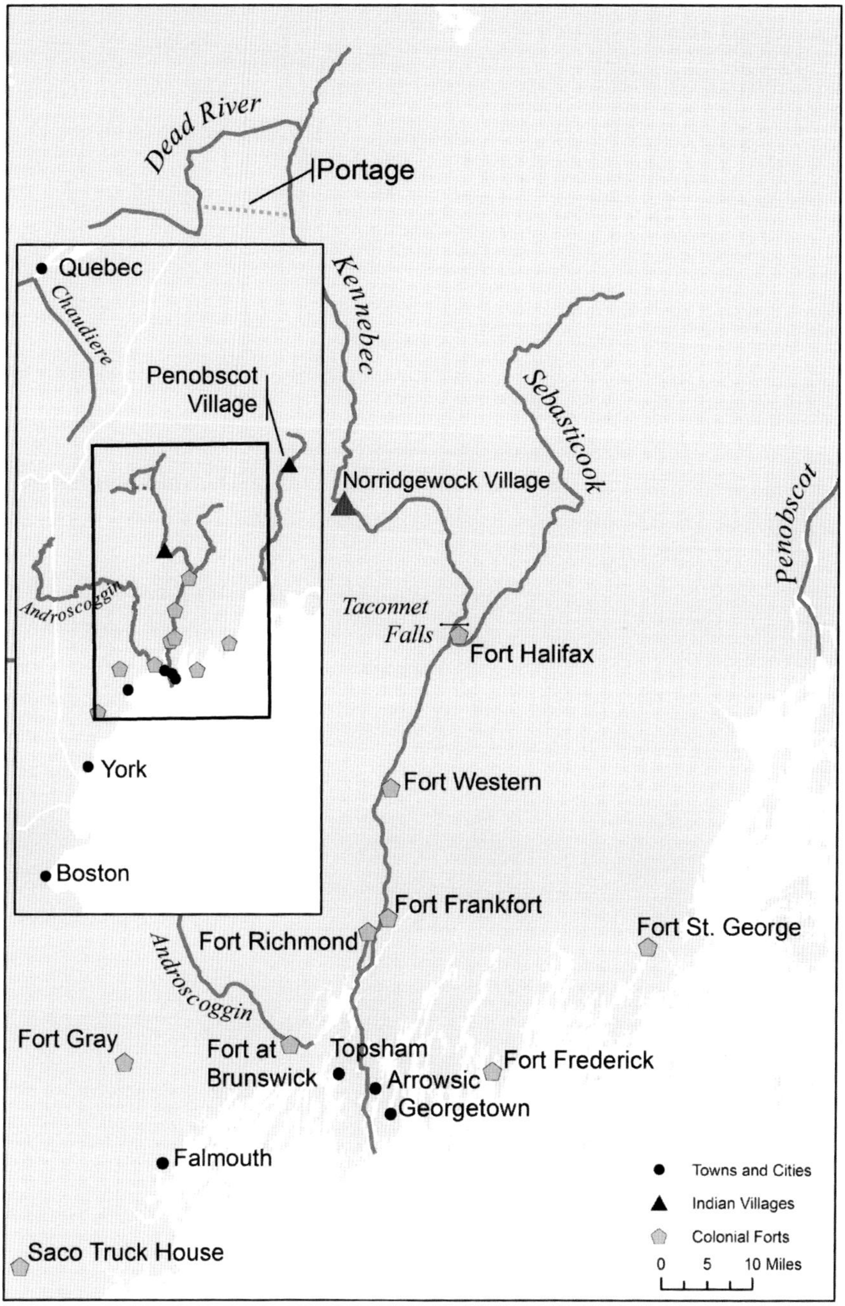

Fort Halifax in 1755. *Manny Gimond.*

Despite these challenges, the commander pursued his orders to fortify and renovate Fort Halifax. He considered rebuilding the entire fort on the hill, one hundred feet above where it currently stood. But he decided that would be too time-consuming and too difficult. On February 14, he submitted his own plans for a smaller and more defensible outpost. Lithgow intended to "entirely alter ye present forme of Fort Hallifax." The captain ordered his men to prepare timber and boards. Crews cut, hauled and then rolled two hundred logs onto a frame. Then, two men operated a pit saw, with one man standing on top of the log and the other in a pit below it. The men also prepared bolts and shingles.[53]

From February to July 1755, Lithgow frequently submitted plans to the governor. He heard nothing. Though he worried that the fort would be "as irregular ill formed assemblage of buildings as was ever huddled together to be called a fort," he forged ahead with construction. Not until late June did the Massachusetts Committee of Wars approve Captain Lithgow's plan. By that time, he was almost done.[54]

All the while, he dealt with frustrations. He needed more oxen and more hay. Poorly made boats made transportation difficult. Resupplying the fort diverted precious time and manpower away from building. Lithgow felt understaffed. Soldiers were "Indifferent, and Several Sick," and there was no doctor. Other men, kept on duty beyond the terms of their enlistments, demanded discharge. The supply of new recruits, and even of enlisted men, never met Lithgow's demand.[55]

By July, however, Lithgow had dramatically overhauled Winslow's plan. High on the hill, overlooking the fort, sat two redoubts, a second one added by Lithgow. Winslow's blockhouse remained. But it now sat at the northeastern corner. Opposite it at the southwestern corner was a new blockhouse. It overlooked a landing on the Sebasticook River. Both blockhouses were two-storied, hip roofed, with dovetailed construction. Both jutted out ten feet beyond the lines of the palisade, offering a better angle for firing against attackers. At the southeast corner of the square was a two-story log sentry box with a hip roof. Most of the eastern side, about one thousand feet from the Kennebec, consisted of a windowless, one-story soldiers' barracks, divided into four buildings. It measured eighty feet long by twenty feet deep, with a shed roof.[56]

On July 15, Governor Shirley ordered Lithgow to reduce the garrison at both forts to a total of eighty men. With construction still ongoing, Lithgow needed workers "[t]o hall Timber Dig stones Burn Brick Cary up workmen" and guards. When Shirley journeyed to the western frontier in the summer

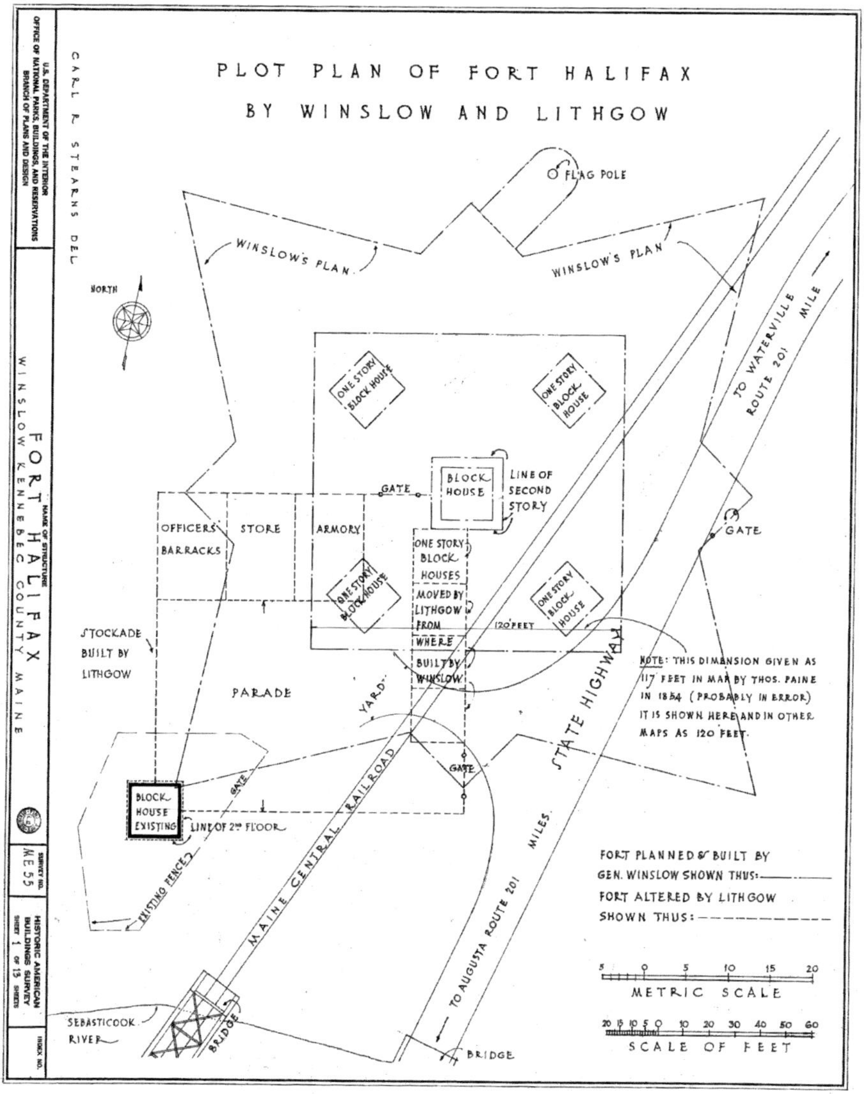

Plot plan of Fort Halifax, by the Historic American Buildings Survey, 1936. *Library of Congress.*

of 1755, Lithgow begged Massachusetts acting governor Spencer Phips for more men, "so that the fort may be completed; for till that time I shall have no peace night or day." He also feared for his men's safety while escorting supplies or dispatches on the Kennebec. But Lithgow obeyed orders. He gradually dismissed men in batches of seven or eight. He first discharged the men who claimed that their "affairs Suffered at ye westward or that their Wives being sick, fathers, Brothers being Dead or Dying and ye lick excuses." Had he "[d]ismissed them all at once, I belive ye garrison would have generly Raised in mutiny, and all gon off." Sixty men remained at Fort Halifax, twenty at Fort Western and ten at Richmond to guard the stores.[57] In mid-August, Massachusetts legislators finally acted on Lithgow's request and authorized Phips to send thirty additional militiamen from New Boston (today Gray, Maine) to Frankfort. They were to escort provisions to Fort Halifax and to guard the workmen on duty.[58]

With fewer soldiers working, but with guardsmen present, construction continued on the largest structure of the fort complex. In the northwestern corner and running more than half of the northern side was the two-story, 40- by 80-foot "Fort House," completed in October 1755. It housed Lithgow's quarters on the north end, and officers' quarters on the south end. A storeroom and the armory filled the space between. Goods were stored in cellars below. On the side of the structure facing the center of the

Engraving of Fort Halifax, by Russell B. Richardson, circa 1876. *Maine Historical Society*.

fort was an overhanging roof. Sentries manned a catwalk on the rooftop. In total, Lithgow's fort was about 120 feet square. Spaces between the buildings were filled by an oak-log palisade, 9½ feet tall. There were two gates. The buildings were not yet weatherproof and would not be until 1756. Lithgow sent the governor an estimate for materials, preparation and installation of ten thousand clapboards, forty-six window caps for small glass windows in the Fort House, casings for thirty-two ports and lookouts and ten doors. A pine flagpole was installed near the southwest corner of the southwest blockhouse. It flew a British Red Ensign flag. Inside the fort was a well, reportedly 80 feet deep, but the water was bad. Soldiers instead used a shallow well outside the fort, about 250 feet to the north. An outhouse was also north of the fort. Fort Halifax was nearly finished.[59]

With Lithgow's efforts, and the cooperation of the Massachusetts Assembly and the governor, Fort Halifax soon amassed a large arsenal. One cannon, which the soldiers affectionately named "the old sow," fired twelve-pound shot, a cannonball four and a half inches in diameter. Two nine-pounder guns served as "alarm guns." Soldiers discharged them to signify danger or for militiamen to arm. Small cannons and swivel guns were placed in the upper stories of the lower blockhouses. Fort Halifax also had at least five cohorn mortars. These small brass pieces were mounted on portable wooden blocks, between handles. They lobbed two-and-three-quarter-inch bombshells.[60] In addition to these artillery pieces, two bulldogs guarded the entrances to the fort.[61]

The fort was mostly done and was well armed by October 1755. But as the captain admitted to his carpenter, Aaron Willard, building it had inflicted the only "fatigue and hardship I have under gon" in twenty years of service to the province. Lithgow's headaches continued.[62] Soldier John Morrison drowned on November 18. Some men had served eighteen difficult months on the harsh Maine frontier. They grew restless and demanded their discharge papers. Lithgow sympathized with them in a letter to acting governor Spencer Phips: "Their Dutey is so much harder then at other Forts."[63]

For the Indians, construction of the fort offered both opportunities and difficulties. A Kennebec Indian named Bartholomew served as a paid guide and pilot for four weeks in early 1755. From December 1754 to February 1766, Massachusetts ran a truck house, a trading post where Indians could exchange furs for supplies and could have their guns repaired.[64] Indians were frequent visitors to Fort Halifax, where they sought trade goods and hospitality and also stopped at Fort Halifax on their way to and from Boston to meet with the governor and council.[65]

Three-pounder cannon linked to Fort Halifax, donated by H. Paul Rancourt to the Friends of Fort Halifax. *Winslow Public Library.*

But for many Indians, Fort Halifax posed a set of new problems: rapid white settlement and competition for fish and game. Some felt they had been tricked or coerced into signing the treaty at Falmouth and resented Fort Halifax's being built. As construction proceeded on the fort and as tensions escalated between the British and French, many Indians on the frontier sided with the French. The French were fewer in numbers and treated the Indians more kindly. Others launched attacks from Canada. In May 1755, Indians attacked the Kennebec Proprietors' settlement and fort, Frankfort (also called Fort Shirley). They burned a house and killed two people. They also captured a soldier from Fort Western, Edward Whaland, as he carried dispatches to Fort Halifax. Whaland was a prisoner in Canada for over four years. The Massachusetts legislature voted on June 10 to declare war on Abenakis east of the Piscataqua River except the Penobscot. In early September, Lithgow's soldiers saw "Sundry Tracts of Indians" on the western side of the Kennebec and expected that the Indians would fall on the frontier inhabitants. On November 1, after discussions fell through, Massachusetts declared war on the Penobscots, too. Finding the French slow to offer assistance, the Norridgewock Indians sought peace with the British.[66]

In December, a returning captive informed Governor Shirley that an army of five hundred Frenchmen and Indians intended to attack the fort. The governor urged the assemblymen to "secure that Fortress at all Hazards" and to take measures "for Bridling the French and Indians" on the Kennebec. He met with a Canadian mulatto named Prient and began to plan a small expedition against the French settlements along the Chaudière River outside Quebec. Ultimately, the British focused their efforts on the New York and Pennsylvania frontiers. But the specter of Indian attack on the Kennebec loomed large as 1756 began. As the fort neared completion, Indians realized that the English men intended to stay. Historians claim that eleven families settled near the fort almost as soon as it was constructed, but the evidence remains thin.[67]

The winter of 1755–56 passed without Anglo-Abenaki violence. On May 30, 1756, Lithgow considered the fort complete. The colony sought reimbursement from the British government and even proposed that British troops would garrison the fort. But on September 24, 1756, Massachusetts's agent in London wrote that the Crown would not take over the fort. The colony would have to fund and man Fort Halifax on its own.[68]

With Massachusetts troops still on duty, garrison life probably resembled most forts in the British Empire. At most colonial forts, each day at 6:00 a.m. a drummer played reveille and the garrison awoke. Any soldiers not on guard duty at the blockhouses formed for work, cutting firewood, baking and repairing tools and weapons. According to military custom, women lived with the soldiers in the garrison. During the day, women nursed sick soldiers, cleaned and swept the barracks and washed, sewed and repaired clothes. Some women stacked firewood for an extra income.[69]

Soldiers and families ate, socialized or slept in the barracks. A sergeant and a dozen soldiers lived in and manned each of the hill redoubts. Rations might have included fresh fish, bread or biscuits, salted beef or pork, peas, butter and potatoes. Lithgow grew potatoes, and there likely were small garden plots at Fort Halifax. Each soldier received a daily allowance of rum. At night, people sat by firelight, singing, dancing, playing the jaw harp and telling stories. Furniture was sparse in most frontier forts: four- by six-foot bunk beds with straw-stuffed mattresses, a wooden table and benches. Gun rags and wooden pegs might have hung from unfinished wooden walls. Barracks probably had basic fireplace implements, a broom, a bucket, a hatchet, pots and kettles, bowls, large plates called trenchers and maybe some pitchers and mugs for beer, cider or spruce beer. Bedtime was at 10:00 p.m. Soldiers slept two to a bed. Like many frontier outposts, families often lived alongside the soldiers. Married couples often bunked together, tacking up sheets for privacy. Children either slept in their parents' beds or on straw mattresses on the floor. Women washed the sheets only once a month; waking up at 6:00 a.m. to begin the routine anew, one hoped the "itch" from the mites that burrowed into the dirty linens was minimal.[70]

Life at Fort Halifax was a family affair. In 1756, Lithgow shut down Fort Richmond and brought his parents, his wife and several small children to Fort Halifax. Lithgow's father, Robert, now nearing seventy, served as a sergeant and "centinell" at Fort Halifax. According to family history, Lithgow's mother "would sit in the attic at Fort Halifax," telling "tales of the old country as she spun her flax on the little wheel."[71]

The captain's sons, Robert Jr. and William Jr., each served at Fort Halifax as a "centinel" and as a drummer. William Jr. first appears on the muster rolls at age eight. Fort Halifax had several sets of brothers, including Ezekiel and Benjamin Pattee. There were several father-and-son enlistees, including James Coller Jr. and Sr. Samuel Howard's nephews served under his brother, James, at Fort Western. The core of the garrison knew one another well; some accompanied Lithgow from Fort Richmond and stayed together at Fort Halifax for several years. Before 1760, as many as a dozen African Americans and "servants"—likely one and the same—also served at Fort Halifax. Most noteworthy was Chubb, a soldier from 1756 to 1758. Cuff and York served at Fort Western. Little is known of these men. They were paid equal wages and shared in the struggles and adventures of fort life.[72]

By late 1756, life seemed more settled. And Lithgow had eighteen months of supplies stored comfortably in the fort.[73] But the soldiers again became discontented. In the summer of 1756, Lithgow feared that many of the soldiers would desert, perhaps with force, "as some have already threatnd (if they should not be discharg'd)." The difficulty of enlisting men to serve on the frontiers, and the difficulties of transportation, necessitated keeping soldiers at Fort Halifax beyond the terms of their enlistments. Some men had been at the fort for two years and must have felt trapped. Governor Shirley asked the Massachusetts Assembly to increase the enlistment bounty to make it resemble the payment for soldiers signing up for the British provincial campaigns in New York. Shirley authorized Lithgow to draft forty-three militiamen from lower York County, Maine, to replace those entitled to a discharge.[74]

Less than two weeks after Lithgow declared the fort complete, any sense of security soon ended. In early June 1756, two brothers from Fort Halifax, Samuel and Robert Barrett, were fishing at the falls within sight of the nearest hill blockhouse. Four Indians opened fire on them and wounded both men. A soldier returned fire, injuring an Indian. Alerted by the sound of guns, men from the garrison sprang into action. As Fort Western's commander, Lieutenant James Howard, reported, the soldiers "[i]ssued out so Quick that they [the Indians] had no Time to Scalp them." Robert Barrett recovered. The next muster roll indicates that Samuel Barrett was "[k]illed by the Indians." His last day of pay was June 13, 1756, the day of his death.[75]

Hostilities flared again in May 1757. Soldiers heard Indians yelling about five miles north of the fort and then spotted rafts drifting by the fort. Captain Lithgow assumed that the Indians used these rafts to "ferry themselves across" the Kennebec and imagined that they had proceeded downriver. He sent an express boat with ten men, led by Ensign Ezekiel Pattee, to warn the settlements of a possible Indian attack.[76]

On May 18, as Pattee and his detachment were returning from Fort Western to Fort Halifax, chaos ensued. Newspaper accounts and military correspondence reveal what happened that day. Pattee "put two Men ashore, as an Advance Guard." About halfway between the two forts, the guardsmen spotted at least seventeen Indians "being within 15 or 20 yards of them & ye Boat." The guardsmen then "[c]ryd out Indains Indains!" One of the soldiers leapt into the river and swam to the boat. The other hid under a root along the riverbank. He would reach Fort Western that night. The parties exchanged three volleys, with the Indians shooting first. Two boatmen suffered multiple gunshot wounds. An Indian fell dead on the riverbank, and another suffered minor wounds. The soldiers retreated across the river, landed the boat and sheltered themselves behind trees. The Indians retreated over a hill and disappeared, carrying their dead comrade and the wounded man "off on their Backs."[77]

After regrouping, the soldiers boarded their boat. They headed south to inform Fort Western of what had happened. They brought Lieutenant John Howard with them and proceeded downriver to Frankfort for medical care. At the fort there, Captain Samuel Goodwin, "haveing ye Remains of a Docters Box which I Gott Last year of my own," treated the injured men and "[d]ressed them in the best Manner I Could."[78]

With the British defeats at Oswego in 1756 and at Fort William Henry in 1757—the latter eventually popularized in the book and movie *The Last of the Mohicans*—Massachusetts's governor and Captain Lithgow, always the optimist, feared that the French and the Indians would target the Maine frontier. Massachusetts legislators hoped "to reduce the Garrison at Fort Halifax to thirty Men" and twelve officers. Governor Thomas Pownall, just arrived to replace Shirley, questioned this plan. "I shall never think it safe to trust that Fort to so small a Number," he said. Captain Lithgow wrote to Pownall on February 16, 1758: "I have bin (and am) verry apprehensive of an attack from ye Enemy." The assembly instead set the troop strength at forty-nine men. Lithgow held his men "in as grate Rediness as Possible." No attack took place. Yet the soldiers lived in fear, Margaret Pattee later recalled. They often "thought they saw or heard the Indians," Elizabeth Freeman recalls her mother saying. They were spooked by shadows in the night, by Indians' stray dogs and by other signs of Indians.[79]

Massachusetts recognized the difficulty of serving at Fort Halifax and attempted to reward the soldiers there. From June 1756 to June 1759, the enlistment bounty increased from two, to three to five pounds. In 1758, Fort Halifax soldier Richard George and others petitioned the assembly. The legislators recognized the "extraordinary duty they are obliged to perform" and increased the soldiers' pay. Still, the supply of soldiers never met the demand. Soldiers were forced to stay on past the terms of their enlistments, and the assembly frequently authorized Captain Lithgow to force men into duty.[80]

Fear of Indian attack had kept settlers from the area. All that changed as British and colonial troops defeated the French and their Indian allies. In July 1759, the British captured Fort Ticonderoga and Fort Niagara. In September, the British defeated the French on the Plains of Abraham and took Quebec. Six soldiers and a guide from Fort Halifax participated with Lieutenant Nathaniel Hutchins of Rogers's Rangers in covert missions against the Abenakis. Later that year, Rogers and his special forces destroyed a village of Abenakis at St. Francis, Quebec—many of the inhabitants there were refugees, migrants or family members of warriors from the Kennebec region. As 1760 dawned, observers believed that the British would soon drive the French from North America.[81]

It was no surprise, then, that the first settlers came to the region between Fort Western and Fort Halifax around 1760. The recruiting efforts of the Kennebec Proprietors also played a critical role. The proprietors published a one-page "broadside" on February 16, 1760, and placed it as an ad in Boston newspapers. The proprietors sought 160 families to settle in two townships created around the two forts within the next two years. "The Land is good," the broadside promised, "well stock'd with Wood and Timber." The Kennebec River, easily navigable up to Fort Western, "abounds with Fish." Settlers could make "a good deal of Money" in just "a few Weeks of the Spring and Fall" by hunting beaver and trapping animals for fur. "Each family would have two hundred acres," rent-free, provided they each build a house, clear and farm the land and dwell there for seven or more years. Other amenities included churches, ministers, muster fields and cemeteries.[82]

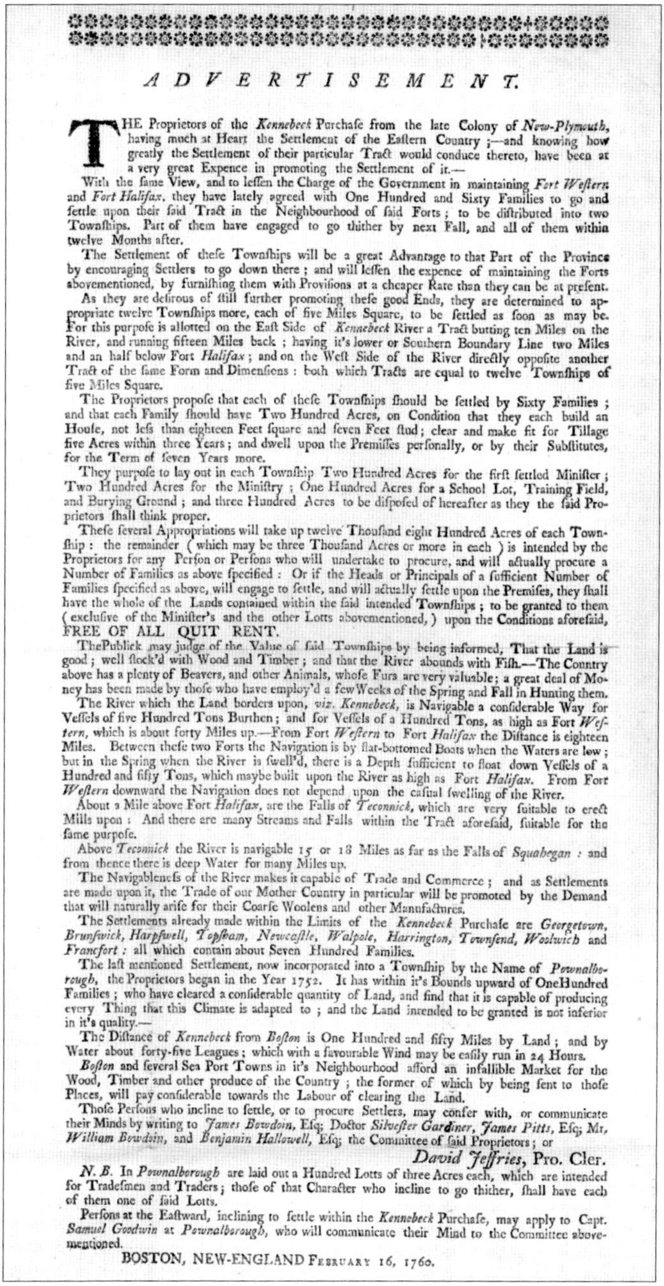

ADVERTISEMENT.

THE Proprietors of the *Kennebeck* Purchaſe from the late Colony of *New-Plymouth*, having much at Heart the Settlement of the Eaſtern Country ;—and knowing how greatly the Settlement of their particular Tract would conduce thereto, have been at a very great Expence in promoting the Settlement of it.—

With the ſame View, and to leſſen the Charge of the Government in maintaining *Fort Weſtern* and *Fort Halifax*, they have lately agreed with One Hundred and Sixty Families to go and ſettle upon their ſaid Tract in the Neighbourhood of ſaid Forts ; to be diſtributed into two Townſhips. Part of them have engaged to go thither by next Fall, and all of them within twelve Months after.

The Settlement of theſe Townſhips will be a great Advantage to that Part of the Province by encouraging Settlers to go down there ; and will leſſen the expence of maintaining the Forts abovementioned, by furniſhing them with Proviſions at a cheaper Rate than they can be at preſent.

As they are deſirous of ſtill further promoting theſe good Ends, they are determined to appropriate twelve Townſhips more, each of five Miles Square, to be ſettled as ſoon as may be. For this purpoſe is allotted on the Eaſt Side of *Kennebeck* River a Tract butting ten Miles on the River, and running fifteen Miles back ; having it's lower or Southern Boundary Line two Miles and an half below Fort *Halifax* ; and on the Weſt Side of the River directly oppoſite another Tract of the ſame Form and Dimenſions : both which Tracts are equal to twelve Townſhips of five Miles Square.

The Proprietors propoſe that each of theſe Townſhips ſhould be ſettled by Sixty Families ; and that each Family ſhould have Two Hundred Acres, on Condition that they each build an Houſe, not leſs than eighteen Feet ſquare and ſeven Feet ſtud ; clear and make fit for Tillage five Acres within three Years ; and dwell upon the Premiſſes perſonally, or by their Subſtitutes, for the Term of ſeven Years more.

They purpoſe to lay out in each Townſhip Two Hundred Acres for the firſt ſettled Miniſter ; Two Hundred Acres for the Miniſtry ; One Hundred Acres for a School Lot, Training Field, and Burying Ground ; and three Hundred Acres to be diſpoſed of hereafter as they the ſaid Proprietors ſhall think proper.

Theſe ſeveral Appropriations will take up twelve Thouſand eight Hundred Acres of each Townſhip : the remainder (which may be three Thouſand Acres or more in each) is intended by the Proprietors for any Perſon or Perſons who will undertake to procure, and will actually procure a Number of Families as above ſpecified : Or if the Heads or Principals of a ſufficient Number of Families ſpecified as above, will engage to ſettle, and will actually ſettle upon the Premiſes, they ſhall have the whole of the Lands contained within the ſaid intended Townſhips ; to be granted to them (excluſive of the Miniſter's and the other Lotts abovementioned,) upon the Conditions aforeſaid, FREE OF ALL QUIT RENT.

The Publick may judge of the Value of ſaid Townſhips by being informed, That the Land is good ; well ſtock'd with Wood and Timber ; and that the River abounds with Fiſh.—The Country above has a plenty of Beavers, and other Animals, whoſe Furs are very valuable ; a great deal of Money has been made by thoſe who have employ'd a few Weeks of the Spring and Fall in Hunting them.

The River which the Land borders upon, *viz. Kennebeck,* is Navigable a conſiderable Way for Veſſels of five Hundred Tons Burthen ; and for Veſſels of a Hundred Tons, as high as Fort *Weſtern*, which is about forty Miles up.—From Fort *Weſtern* to Fort *Halifax* the Diſtance is eighteen Miles. Between theſe two Forts the Navigation is by flat-bottomed Boats when the Waters are low ; but in the Spring when the River is ſwell'd, there is a Depth ſufficient to float down Veſſels of a Hundred and fifty Tons, which maybe built upon the River as high as Fort *Halifax*. From Fort *Weſtern* downward the Navigation does not depend upon the caſual ſwelling of the River.

About a Mile above Fort *Halifax*, are the Falls of *Teconnick*, which are very ſuitable to erect Mills upon : And there are many Streams and Falls within the Tract aforeſaid, ſuitable for the ſame purpoſe.

Above *Teconnick* the River is navigable 15 or 18 Miles as far as the Falls of *Squabegan* : and from thence there is deep Water for many Miles up.

The Navigableneſs of the River makes it capable of Trade and Commerce ; and as Settlements are made upon it, the Trade of our Mother Country in particular will be promoted by the Demand that will naturally ariſe for their Coarſe Woolens and other Manufactures.

The Settlements already made within the Limits of the *Kennebeck* Purchaſe are *Georgetown, Brunſwick, Harpſwell, Topſham, Newcaſtle, Walpole, Harrington, Townſend, Woolwich* and *Francfort* : all which contain about Seven Hundred Families.

The laſt mentioned Settlement, now incorporated into a Townſhip by the Name of *Pownalborough,* the Proprietors began in the Year 1752. It has within it's Bounds upward of One Hundred Families ; who have cleared a conſiderable quantity of Land, and find that it is capable of producing every Thing that this Climate is adapted to ; and the Land intended to be granted is not inferior in it's quality.—

The Diſtance of *Kennebeck* from *Boſton* is One Hundred and fifty Miles by Land ; and by Water about forty-five Leagues ; which with a favourable Wind may be eaſily run in 24 Hours.

Boſton and ſeveral Sea Port Towns in it's Neighbourhood afford an infallible Market for the Wood, Timber and other produce of the Country ; the former of which by being ſent to thoſe Places, will pay conſiderable towards the Labour of clearing the Land.

Thoſe Perſons who incline to ſettle, or to procure Settlers, may confer with, or communicate their Minds by writing to *James Bowdoin*, Eſq; Doctor *Silveſter Gardiner*, *James Pitts*, Eſq; Mr. *William Bowdoin*, and *Benjamin Hallowell*, Eſq; the Committee of ſaid Proprietors ; or

David Jeffries, Pro. Cler.

N. B. In *Pownalborough* are laid out a Hundred Lotts of three Acres each, which are intended for Tradeſmen and Traders ; thoſe of that Character who incline to go thither, ſhall have each of them one of ſaid Lotts.

Perſons at the Eaſtward, inclining to ſettle within the *Kennebeck* Purchaſe, may apply to Capt. *Samuel Goodwin* at *Pownalborough*, who will communicate their Mind to the Committee abovementioned.

BOSTON, NEW-ENGLAND FEBRUARY 16, 1760.

Advertisement by the Kennebec Proprietors, February 16, 1760. *Maine Historical Society*.

As settlers eyed the Kennebec in 1760, Massachusetts legislators subdivided Maine's vast York County. Cumberland County encompassed the region between the Saco River and the Kennebec River. All communities east were now part of the new Lincoln County. Captain Lithgow and Lieutenant James Howard of Fort Western became justices of the peace. Lithgow also became a militia colonel. Frankfort was renamed Pownalborough, after Massachusetts's governor. In 1761, the Kennebec Proprietors tore down the fort there and built Pownalborough Courthouse. Lithgow was commissioned a judge of the Court of Common Pleas of Lincoln County. Each summer, court was in session at the new courthouse. John Adams argued a case there in 1765.[83]

After the peace with France, British surveyors also gained a firmer grasp of the geography of Maine. In August 1761, the now British governor of Canada sent a crew, led by engineer John Montresor, to map and explore the region between Quebec City and Fort Halifax. The previous year, he had

Colonel John Montresor, by John Singleton Copley, circa 1771. *Detroit Institute of the Arts/ Bridgeman Library*.

traveled from Quebec up the Chaudière River to the Dead River and then down the Androscoggin River to Topsham, Maine.[84] This year, he descended the Kennebec to Fort Halifax and then to return to Quebec.

Montresor arrived by canoe on July 7, 1761. He wrote in his journal, "We came to Ticonic Falls, which are immediately above Fort Halifax. We left our canoes above the falls and went into the fort." He and his men visited for two days. He described the fort as "a bad palisade, (flanked) by two blockhouses, in which there are some guns mounted." He noted that the fort "is commanded by a rising ground behind it." The blockhouses offered little protection against artillery but "are more than sufficient against an enemy who has no other defensive weapon than small arms." The garrison, he observed, depended on the "settlements below" for supplies. Montresor took a small detachment of soldiers led by James Howard, commander of Fort Western, from Fort Halifax for the return trip to Quebec. About 120 miles north of the fort, one of his party "perceived a rustling" in the bushes and shot what turned out to be an Indian.[85] In 1764, another surveying expedition under Joseph Chadwick traveled from Fort Pownall, built in 1760 in what is today Fort Point State Park. They journeyed down the Sebasticook to Fort Halifax.[86] In 1775, American troops under Benedict Arnold would use the maps, journals and correspondence of these surveyors, along with materials from Samuel Goodwin at Pownalborough, to trace a route to Quebec.

Peace on the Kennebec also meant a continued transformation for Fort Halifax. Fort Halifax consistently had the largest garrison of any of Massachusetts's forts, but its manpower was gradually reduced after 1760. Life at Fort Halifax also lightened up a little. Lithgow had the soldiers sweep the ice off the river "and slide the ladies," Ezekiel Pattee later told his daughter Elizabeth. Lithgow arranged for excursions on an island near Taconnet Falls with "a very large, basswood tree on it, where the officers and their wives had suppers." Soldiers fired the twelve-pounder cannon "when they had good news, and for sport" and "to frighten" Indian guests, she reported. Sometimes the bombs burst in the air; on other occasions, they landed in the woods across the Kennebec in what is today Waterville. The men wagered their liquor rations in target practice.[87] Romances blossomed, and weddings took place at Fort Halifax. Soldier Michael Maharn married Unis Tarr of Georgetown on August 20, 1761. Lithgow performed the ceremony.[88]

The fort also supported the wave of newly arrived settlers. In 1764, Morris Fling, once a soldier at Fort Richmond and Fort Western, became the first farmer near the fort. He cleared land around it and grew potatoes and corn. Two years later, in March 1766, the Plymouth Company gave

18,600 acres of land in present-day Winslow and Waterville to proprietor Major General John Winslow and five associates with the goal of promoting settlement. Fifty lots were sold to single and married men, and a community soon began to develop.[89]

For Indians, the arrival of settlers impinged on already shrinking hunting grounds and endangered lives and livelihoods. New settlers and renegade fur trappers often viewed the few remaining Indian inhabitants of the upper Kennebec with disdain. Colonial newspapers spread rumors and

Abenaki couple, circa 1750–80. *City of Montreal Archives.*

hysteria. Indians pleaded with Captain Lithgow to protect them. Some even threatened violence. One visitor found how sympathetic Lithgow was. He "made some threatning [*sic*] words," Lithgow wrote in March 1764. Then "I knocked him off the Chair…caught him fast by the Throat." The captain continued his attack, slamming the Indian's head against the chimney jam, drawing blood. He then "seized him by the Neck…and dragged him out side…gave him a kick or two on his Britch" and sent him on his way. Indians found that their concerns no longer mattered, and they had no legal or physical rights.[90]

In 1765, reports had stated that "[t]wo Indians were found burnt to Death, in their Camp, near Fort Halifax," perhaps the victims of arson.[91] White hunters murdered a Norridgewock chief and his wife on Cobboseecontee Pond in present-day Winthrop that fall and then plundered the wigwam's possessions. Massachusetts governor Francis Bernard offered a £100 reward to any person or persons who "discover the Author or Authors of the said Mischief." He ordered Lithgow to provide the victim's family with two guns, twenty beaver skins, blankets and beads as restitution. Lithgow never solved

The Lithgow family plot in the Lithgow-Morse Cemetery, Phippsburg, Maine. *Author photo.*

the murder.[92] The following year, another Indian family was found dead in southern Maine. Informants later implicated Daniel Austin, a former soldier at Fort Halifax from 1754 to 1756.[93]

In May 1766, a committee of the House of Representatives opined "that it is not expedient to continue the Trade at Fort Halifax." The garrison, and that of Fort Western, which had been gradually reduced since 1761, and stood at just thirteen men, total, was disbanded the following year. The Lithgows relocated to Georgetown, now Phippsburg. Sarah and William had three more children, for a total of eleven.[94] Colonel Lithgow died in 1798 at his farm. He was buried in a nearby field with a simple gravestone.[95]

After 1767, the fort was no longer needed. As Harry Mitchell and B.V. Davis wrote in 1904, "The purpose of the fort was now realized. It was the key to the region of the Kennebec, and had unlocked the valley to the axe of the settler."[96] In Lithgow's twelve years at Fort Halifax, power had shifted from the French and the Indians to the British settlers, who arrived in increasing numbers in central Maine. But the fort, and what remained of it, would remain the center of life in the region. It would also figure prominently in the Revolutionary era.

Chapter 4

A Tory, an Army and a Truck House, 1770–1785

Rhode Island–born Dr. Silvester Gardiner received the finest training in New York, London and Paris. He practiced medicine and ran a pharmacy in Boston and lectured on anatomy in his spare time. A pioneer in smallpox inoculation, he founded a hospital. He was also a land developer and promoter. As a member of the Plymouth Company, Dr. Gardiner was deeply involved with the proprietors' lands on the Kennebec. It is no surprise, then, that as settlement increased in the region around and above Fort Halifax in the late 1760s, Dr. Gardiner saw a new opportunity and sprang into action. On July 4, 1770, Massachusetts sold Fort Halifax. Gardiner paid £160 for the fort and £400 for the adjoining acres. He then leased the property, which included a tavern in the former officers' barracks.[97]

Fort Halifax no longer had its garrison, but it remained a prominent landmark, and it bore witness to an exciting history in the Revolutionary era. By 1770, the Kennebec Proprietors had obtained fifty settlers, twenty-five of whom had families. Life revolved around the fort and the protection that it offered. As settlers arrived from Massachusetts, they sometimes stayed at the fort before setting up their homesteads.[98]

Until 1771, all the surrounding lands from Taconnet Falls, including Waterville, Winslow and Oakland, were called Kingsfield. As pro-monarchy sentiment waned, in April 1771, the Massachusetts Assembly established the town of Winslow, named in honor of Major General John Winslow.[99] May 23, 1771, marked the date of the first town meeting, held in the Fort House. Ezekiel Pattee, the ensign in command during the May

Dr. Silvester Gardiner, by John Singleton Copley, circa 1772. *Seattle Art Museum.*

1757 skirmish on the Kennebec, became the town's first first selectman. He would later serve as town clerk and treasurer.[100] Pattee and his wife, Margaret, were married in Georgetown in 1760. They eventually had eleven children. Several were born during the several years that the family lived in one of the hill blockhouses. Ezekiel Pattee ran a tavern at Fort Halifax and served as a captain in the local militia. In the 1770s, the town contracted with ministers to hold religious services in the second floor of the Fort House. The Reverends John Murray of Boothbay, Jacob Bailey and Deliverance Smith preached at Fort Halifax.[101]

Fort Halifax remained a base for surveying expeditions, as well, just as it had for John Montresor and Joseph Chadwick in the 1760s. In 1773, an expedition under Surveyor General Hugh Finley set out from Quebec, intending "to steer a direct course through the woods from Sartigan" to Fort Halifax, "in order to ascertain the uninhabited distance, and to estimate the expence of opening a post road that way," as well as to survey post roads to the south.[102] The fort remained at the core of the community; in 1772, Gardiner gave land to the town for a cemetery (today's Fort Hill Cemetery on Halifax Street) on the road leading up the hill to one of the redoubts. By 1774, the town had built a new road running north from the fort and cleared another running southeast from Fort Halifax.[103] Improved roads facilitated the rapid development of the region, with Fort Halifax as a hub for the growing community.

In April 1775, British troops and Massachusetts militiamen clashed at Lexington and Concord. In June, the British bombarded Boston. War came to New England. Soon, it came to Fort Halifax. Colonel Benedict Arnold, fresh off of seizing the artillery at British-held Fort Ticonderoga, hatched a plan. The Americans needed to somehow strike a blow against the British and expand the war. So he planned an invasion of Quebec through the

Colonel Benedict Arnold, by Thomas Hart, 1776. *Brown University/Bridgeman Art Library.*

Kennebec-Chaudière corridor. Arnold's army of 1,100 men marched from Cambridge, Massachusetts, to Newburyport. They sailed for the Kennebec on September 18. And by the twenty-first, they had reached the house of Major Reuben Colburn in present-day Pittston, where they loaded up with supplies and two hundred small boats.

When Arnold's troops first arrived, they noticed that the fort had begun to deteriorate. An advance party of Pennsylvanians reached Fort Halifax on September 23. Private John Joseph Henry wrote in his journal that Fort Halifax "consisted of old Block-houses and a stockade in a ruinous state" and "did not admit of much comfort; besides it was inhabited…by a rank tory." Henry and the soldiers lodged in a private residence nearby. They enjoyed "agreeable" conversation and learned of the decline of the area deer population, which must have helped explain why so few Kennebec Indians remained. The next morning, the soldiers returned to the fort and met the Tory, Ephraim Ballard, "who claimed the right of thinking for himself." Ballard, a surveyor, and Silvester Gardiner's tenant and caretaker for the property, traded them a barrel of smoked salmon for a barrel of pork, "upon honest terms," and they proceeded upriver.[104]

As Henry and the Pennsylvanians scouted ahead, the bulk of Arnold's army left Fort Western for Fort Halifax. Some traveled by bateaux. Others walked some, or all, of the rough road on the east bank of the Kennebec that led from Augusta to Winslow. They reached the fort between September 26 and October 1, 1775. Arnold apparently penned a letter to his commissary general on September 29 before leaving Fort Western. The letter carried orders to send all supplies to Fort Halifax "as fast as posable," namely "[a]ll the New Battoes Poles Oars Pitch Nails &c." Major Return Meigs of Connecticut saw "two large block-houses, and a large barrack [the tavern], which is enclosed with a picket fort." As Dr. Isaac Senter put it, "This appeared a very pleasant prospect." But the prospects for the expedition looked grim. Boats were damaged, and men were sick. Senter's bateau arrived "in such a shattered condition" that he had to purchase another. He also noted that "several of our army were much troubled with the dysentery, diarrhea, &c." These were ominous signs of the hardship to come.[105]

The men, most from New England, Pennsylvania and Virginia, arrived in waves and gathered at Fort Halifax before they began the arduous task of hauling their canoes around or over the waterfalls and rapids up the Kennebec River. Officers secured private accommodations in the sparsely populated countryside. Enlisted soldiers camped outside the fort or across the Sebasticook River along present-day Lithgow Street. Many of the soldiers

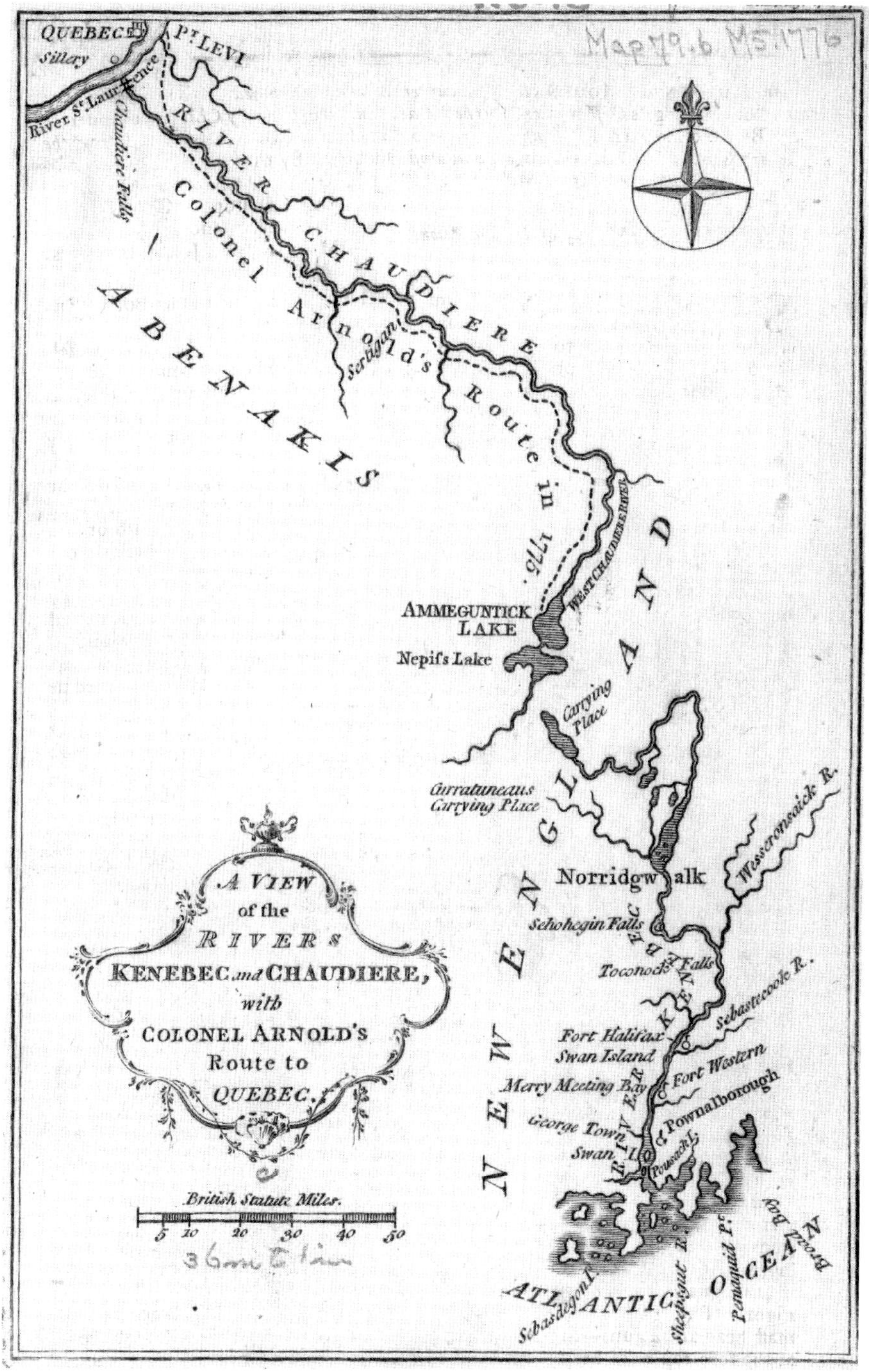

"View of the Rivers Kenebec and Chaudière," by Robert Baldwin, 1776. *Norman B. Leventhal Map Center, Boston Public Library.*

A reproduction bateau, 1975. *The Major Reuben Colburn House.*

who reached Fort Halifax later attained prominence. Henry Dearborn fought at Fort Ticonderoga, Freeman's Farm, Saratoga and Monmouth and served as Thomas Jefferson's secretary of war. Daniel Morgan and his riflemen earned acclaim at the Battle of Cowpens. Indian guides paddled as Arnold rode in a birch bark canoe. Some Indian women even joined. These Indians became the subject of nineteenth-century legend. Traveling with Dr. Senter was General Nathanael Greene's third cousin, Christopher Greene. One of several gentleman volunteers was nineteen-year-old Aaron Burr. Burr later became a lawyer, was U.S. vice president under Thomas Jefferson, shot U.S. Treasury secretary Alexander Hamilton in a duel, allegedly conspired against the United States and garnered a reputation as a womanizer.[106]

As historian Tom Desjardin explains, in 1827, Henry Dearborn, then living in Gardiner, Maine, told an elaborate story—which available documentation does not corroborate—that Aaron Burr seduced Jacataqua, an Indian princess from Swan Island in the Kennebec, impregnated her and brought her with him on the expedition to Canada. This story, and several versions of it, took on a life of its own and appeared in numerous forms, most notably in Kenneth Roberts's novel of the Arnold campaign, *Arundel*. Nonetheless, Burr was at Fort Halifax in 1775.[107]

Burr's alleged exploits at Fort Halifax became legendary in the mid-nineteenth century. In 1852, Ezekiel Pattee's daughter Elizabeth Freeman recalled that in 1775, Burr visited Fort House Tavern, located inside the fort. "A great many times," she claimed, her father, the tavern keeper, told his guests a memorable story. Much to the chagrin of "an Indian maiden," Jacataqua, the young gentleman "made love to the fair Sarah Lithgow," the daughter of the fort's former commander. The soldier reportedly wrote sonnets "on the bark of the silver birch" that grew by the falls. He sent the poems to her by his servant. But before long, "[s]he would have nothing to do with him." The tale seems dubious. Sarah Lithgow was, at the time, living in Augusta with her husband of nine years, Lieutenant Samuel Howard. Samuel, a trader, was the son of former Fort Western officer John Howard. Nonetheless, the visit of Burr and of Arnold's army is one memorable episode in the rich history of Fort Halifax.[108]

Aaron Burr, attributed to Gilbert Stuart, circa 1793. *From the Collection of the New Jersey Historical Society.*

This was not the last activity at the fort during the Revolutionary years. In 1776, the Winslow selectmen and the Winslow Committee of Safety, the men who organized American resistance on the local level and corresponded with Patriot leaders in Boston, chased the Tory Ephraim Ballard out of town. Upon learning that Dr. Gardiner had fled Boston with British troops, they informed the governor that "Ballard was of Principles inimical to the glorious Cause." They felt "warranted to take the Fort and Land into Possession and lease them out." They visited Ballard "and requested him to deliver them up." He refused, maintaining that he had lawfully leased the property. Three weeks later, townspeople complained that "Mr Ballard with a Number of People (supposed to be unfriendly to the grand American Cause)" from what is today the neighboring town of Vassalboro "were cutting and haling Mill Logs" on fort lands, which were the "property of the State." When a Committee of Safety member again visited Ballard, the Tory insisted that the committee "had no right to interfere in the Business." On April 23, 1776, the Massachusetts legislature promptly authorized the Committee of Safety to seize Fort Halifax. The committee did so and subsequently leased out the property. Ballard relocated to Hallowell and moved his wife, Martha, from Massachusetts to live with him. She became a famous midwife and diarist and inspired a book and film called *A Midwife's Tale*.[109]

When British forces seized control of Penobscot Bay in June 1779, driving settlers and Indians from their homes, Fort Halifax gained new importance. The fort served as a base for scouting parties. In June 1779, British troops seized Castine, a rendezvous for American privateers, and built a fort there. Massachusetts then attempted to drive out the British and launched an expeditionary force called the Penobscot Expedition. Colonel Paul Revere, four years removed from his "midnight ride," commanded the Massachusetts artillery. Ezekiel Pattee served with the militia. In July 1779, Fort Halifax served as a staging area for this Patriot attack on British defenses in Maine's Penobscot Bay. Though Massachusetts troops landed at Castine, they failed to take the British fort. They boarded their ships once again and sailed up the Penobscot River toward Bangor with the British in pursuit. The Americans lost ships and men. Escorted by Penobscot Indians, Revere and hundreds of survivors fled through the woods and then down the Sebasticook, fifty miles to Fort Halifax. He and some weary companions were carried by whaleboat to Fort Western and then to Hallowell, where they boarded ships for Boston.[110]

Just as it had devastated Massachusetts by 1779, the war proved disruptive to the Penobscot Indians. They had already lost four warriors in service to the American cause. In September 1779, Massachusetts created a truck house (trading post) at Fort Halifax to exchange goods for furs with Penobscot Indians and to supply the American-allied warriors. Colonel Josiah Brewer was appointed truck master and received a salary of sixty pounds per month.[111] In 1780, Chief Joseph Orono and some Penobscots brought Brewer and an interpreter to Newport, Rhode Island, to meet with French diplomats. They returned, by way of Boston, with a French priest. They also brought compensation for their widows and fabric, food, gunpowder and musket balls, hatchets and knives. By November 1780, Orono and thirty Indians temporarily settled near Fort Halifax. Using Fort Halifax as a base, Orono delivered dispatches to Machias and to the Micmac, Maliseet and Passamaquoddy tribes, organized Penobscot war and diplomacy and traveled to Boston to advocate for his people.[112]

Penobscot Indians came to Fort Halifax to receive flour, rations and presents from the State of Massachusetts. At Fort Halifax, they traded bear, beaver, fisher, mink, moose, muskrat, otter, raccoon and sable hides for gunpowder, shot, musket balls, tools, knives and hatchets, fish hooks, sewing needles, assorted types of fabric, ribbons, tin kettles, vermillion for red face paint, pork, molasses, butter, tobacco and pipes. A French priest, Father Juniper Berthiaume, ministered to the Penobscots. By one account, Berthiaume "had his house at the mouth of the Mile Brook," today about a mile up the Sebasticook on Garland Road. A Catholic ring was later found at the site of Fort Halifax.[113]

Chief Joseph Orono Powder Horn, circa 1780. *From the Collection of the Abbe Museum.*

The truck house never fulfilled the Indians' expectations. Berthiaume claimed that Brewer defrauded the Indians. The Indians traveled vast distances for better bargains, trading with the British at Castine and in Canada.[114] A false report suggested that Berthiaume was spreading anti-American propaganda. Massachusetts authorities promptly dismissed the priest. Soon, they saw the error of their snap judgment. The Indians protested, and white men, including Ezekiel Pattee, defended "honest" Father Berthiaume. Writing from retirement in Georgetown, Maine, Colonel Lithgow praised the priest for "cultivating a friendly intercourse between the Inhabitants & Indians." Berthiaume traveled to Boston to clear his name, promising the governor "what a revolution would happen if Coll

Brow and his Interpreter were not dismissed and if I was not to continue my functions." After several Indian chiefs came to Boston to press the matter, the legislature reinstated Berthiaume in October 1782. They failed to pay him, however. Eventually, the lawmakers discharged him in 1783, and he returned to France in 1784.[115]

When the legislature reinstated Berthiaume in 1782, it also dismissed Colonel Brewer. But he continued at the fort until March 18, 1783. Only then did he learn of his dismissal. He turned over the stores at the fort to the state. Several months later, he submitted his accounts for reimbursement. He defended his actions by arguing that he had advanced large sums of his own money in service to the state and that his days at the truck house had been difficult to say the least. He had to "procure Sentrys…to keep the Indians in subjection & prevent their rushing into the Store." His three years as truck house manager had caused him "great Trouble and expence."[116]

Despite the controversy, Brewer remained at Fort Halifax after his dismissal. He petitioned the Massachusetts legislature on October 22, 1783. Now, "being destitute of House or Home of his own," he requested "to remain in, and occupy, the Fort House where he now resides, together with about ten Acres of Land adjoining," which he had fenced in. The assembly approved Brewer's petition on March 2, 1784, and allowed him to stay there rent-free for one year. The approved petition stated that if Brewer moved, "it will be improved by the first person that can get the Possession thereof, without ever paying any Rent to the Commonwealth thereof."[117] That person apparently later became tavern keeper Richard Thomas. But a legal error in the confiscation of the doctor's Maine property enabled Dr. Gardiner's son-in-law, Robert Hallowell, to recover it. Hallowell eventually sold the fort to Thomas in 1798.[118]

Meanwhile, white settlement increased rapidly. In October 1780, while the truck house was in operation, the Massachusetts legislature had authorized the Kennebec Proprietors to build a new road and to allot lands on the west side of the Kennebec River, north of Fort Halifax. At the time of Arnold's arrival, just twenty families lived near Fort Halifax. By 1790, Winslow's population had increased to 797, 479 of them across the Kennebec in what became Waterville. Another sixty families from Cape Cod had settled north of the fort, thanks to the new road.[119] The Revolutionary War era had brought new guests and new residents to Fort Point and the surrounding area.

Chapter 5

Relics and Investigations, 1785–1890

Elizabeth Freeman was the eighth of Ezekiel and Mary (Howard) Pattee's eleven children. She was born at Fort Halifax in 1777 while her father was tavern keeper there. Her earliest memories dated back to the early 1780s. "They put me on the roof of the Fort [house]," she recalled, "but did not let me go far because the timbers were decayed." She added, "I have picked cucumbers under the eaves of the Barrack." As the fort's structures fell into disrepair and the needs of local residents shifted, the fort, and Fort Point, transformed. In 1852, a seventy-five-year-old Freeman wandered the ruins of the fort, trying to recall what she had heard and seen in her youth. Little of Fort Halifax remained. In Freeman's childhood, the Fort House was a tavern. Its second floor hosted church services, public meetings, dances and parties and housed poor families. By the end of the eighteenth century, however, Dr. Gardiner's heirs had finally recovered the property and sold it to Richard Thomas. He tore down the Fort House and built the Halifax House, an inn and tavern, in 1798. Most of Fort Halifax had been disassembled or had decayed long before that, though. Freeman's father, Ezekiel Pattee, had disassembled and rafted the hill redoubts a short distance down the Kennebec River to build a new home for his growing family.[120] By 1798, only the blockhouse built by Lithgow on the Sebasticook remained. It was a "fancy goods store."[121] The surviving structure was in poor condition. The blockhouse nearly disappeared, too. Somehow it survived several devastating floods in the early 1800s, floods that washed out bridges and caused severe damage.[122]

Despite its critical condition, Fort Halifax had one last, though accidental, gasp as a military outpost. This came during the War of 1812 (1812–15).

Rumors spread that Penobscot Indians were siding with the British and would attack settlements along Maine's Penobscot and Kennebec Rivers. Then, in September 1814, a British vessel chased an American ship up the Penobscot River. In a scene reminiscent of Massachusetts's 1779 debacle in the Penobscot Expedition, the Americans abandoned ship and fled on foot over land. They traveled from the Penobscot to the Sebasticook River and downstream to Clinton village, a few miles north of Fort Halifax. Several ladies were quilting when they caught a glimpse of the fleeing Americans. They mistook the men for attacking Indians and ran to notify their families. Soon the air was filled with shouting: "The Injuns are coming!" The locals could not tell exactly what was happening, but the "Falls residents decided to take no chances, and all went down to Fort Halifax to fortify against the raid they were sure was coming." Gershom Flagg, the grandson of the builder of Fort Western and Fort Halifax, headed the opposite way to confront the perceived threat head-on.[123]

Entire families fled to the Fort Halifax blockhouse. This whole incident had begun at about noon, but three hours later, news of the potential Indian threat reached Norridgewock on the Kennebec River. Not until midnight did the truth become known. The so-called Indians were actually Americans fleeing from a more powerful British ship. Afterward, "the frightened settlers made their way back home from Fort Halifax."[124] Despite the passage of time and the abuse it had endured from its own citizens, Fort Point, connected by roads and history, was still a strategic area to gather in a time of crisis.

After the "Clinton Raid," as the event came to be known, Fort Halifax—reduced to a lone blockhouse with a nearby inn—resumed its shift toward neglect imposed by economic change. Writer Edward Augustus Kendall described this transitional phase in his *Travels through the Northern Parts of the United States*. In 1808, by ferry, he reached the remains of Fort Halifax, where Halifax House inn now stood. From there, he observed Taconnet Falls, "a cataract of remarkable beauty." Yet sawmills and gristmills—including Asa Redington's—dotted the surrounding landscape at the falls in Winslow and in the village to the west, today known as Waterville. Shipbuilding factories churned out partly finished vessels and sent them downriver.[125] As the area grew rapidly, the property once occupied by the fort changed hands several times in the early 1800s, and Fort Halifax and its remnant faded in significance. At the same time, a new college, which later became Colby College, opened in Waterville in 1818. And Maine split off from Massachusetts in 1820 and became the twenty-third state.

By the 1840s, the first railroad line came through Winslow. Workers dug up the fort's southeastern corner and lay tracks over the imprint of the fort.[126]

Some individuals still saw the value in the remaining blockhouse and in the rich history of Fort Halifax. The first and most noteworthy of these was Timothy Otis Paine. He was born in the Paine House, today located on China Road within sight of the blockhouse, on October 13, 1824. Timothy attended school at the one-room Fort Halifax School on Lithgow Street—which afforded a view of the blockhouse across the lower Sebasticook. A promising student, young Timothy attended Waterville College. There he adopted some strange habits. He showered daily during a time period when it was not common to do so. He abstained from alcohol and joined a local temperance society. Paine, a vegetarian, also abstained from milk and butter and frequently bragged of the health benefits he enjoyed: "The result of all of this [is] that my countenance is more healthy, body more stronger [*sic*] and mind far more clear and glad."[127] He even walked all but three miles from Bangor to Winslow—a fifty-mile trip. The bookish and eccentric Winslow native Timothy Paine graduated college in 1847 and became a traveling artist.[128]

On May 23, 1848, tragedy struck. During the maiden voyage of the steamship *Halifax*, affectionately named for the blockhouse and built in the Waterville shipyards, something went terribly wrong: "In passing through the lock in the [newly built] dam at Augusta the boiler exploded." Eight men were killed, including Timothy's brother Charles, who had designed the boiler and served as the ship's master.[129] Timothy memorialized his brother in a portrait. A few years later, he moved to Massachusetts and became a minister. Paine later became a scholar of antiquity. He wrote several books, including *Solomon's Temple*. At one time, it was the "largest and finest book" in the Colby College Library, according to the *Colby Echo*.[130]

Timothy Paine drew on his childhood memories, his scholarly skills, his fascination with Winslow history and his drawing skills. In hopes of erasing the negative association of Fort Halifax with the steamship disaster that took his brother's life, he rescued the fort from obscurity. In the early 1850s, he conducted valuable historical, architectural and archaeological investigations at and around the remaining blockhouse of Fort Halifax and produced a series of sketches. In doing so, he relied heavily on now seventy-five-year-old Elizabeth Freeman's memories and validation. Widowed at twenty-nine, she had never remarried. Paine published his findings in four editions of the *Eastern Mail* in late 1852. His reports shed light on the design of the fort and detailed the history of the surviving blockhouse. He also uncovered countless artifacts left by Indians and soldiers alike. He found arrowheads and tomahawks, earrings, copper beads and pestles. He found cannonballs, shot and bullets, rings, pipes, fort keys and even the spade used to dig the palisade. He sketched the fort as it must have looked in 1756 and submitted an amended report to the Maine Historical Society in 1855. He drew the complex with "such perfection," his brother Albert Ware Paine wrote, that Mrs. Freeman responded "with exclamations of delight" and agreed that it was an accurate portrayal of Fort Halifax as she remembered it as a child.[131]

First, Paine located, measured and detailed the outline of the fort and its various components. He also located the remains of two chimneys. He discovered that the Fort House had a cellar for private storage. Even in 1852, "the Cellar walls of the Fort House are nearly as perfect as they were ninety years ago." He estimated that each side of Fort Halifax had been 117 feet square. He concluded that "[a]lthough the design of the Fort was admirable…it could have afforded but feeble resistance to even a small band of reckless soldiers." He considered it "in fact impregnable to [the Indians] unless they cut off supplies." The French never attacked, Paine believed, because "they were called to more important posts; and the Indians were too wise to attack it." Paine found the remnants of two wells. He also found a flagpole and an outhouse.[132]

Paine continued his investigations, tracing the road that led from the main fort to the blockhouses on the hill, today's Halifax Street. Freeman helped to convince Paine that despite John Montresor's 1761 account, there had actually been a third blockhouse on the hill. "Mrs. Freeman, when asked if there had only been two blockhouses upon the hillside, answered; 'No! There were not two but there were three.'"[133] Though this was incorrect, Paine's findings nonetheless preserved many valuable insights about the fort.

Second, he chronicled the history of Fort Halifax's surviving blockhouse. It was used as a fancy goods store by "a Scotchman" named William Pitt. It remains unclear when Pitt operated his fancy goods store, but it was around the time that Richard Thomas had constructed his Halifax House in 1798. Pitt made several changes, according to Freeman: "A window was cut in the first story, a stair way cut through the chamber-floor, and a chimney built in the South East corner (there had been one in the second floor previously). He also added stairs down on the outside." Pitt gave Mrs. Freeman "a pair of kid gloves when [she] was a young lady."[134]

Paine also commented on the poor condition of the blockhouse. Upon close inspection, the modern history buff might notice indentations from bullets in the original timbers of the old blockhouse. As Paine noted, most of the bullet holes appear on the first level, suggesting shots fired inside the

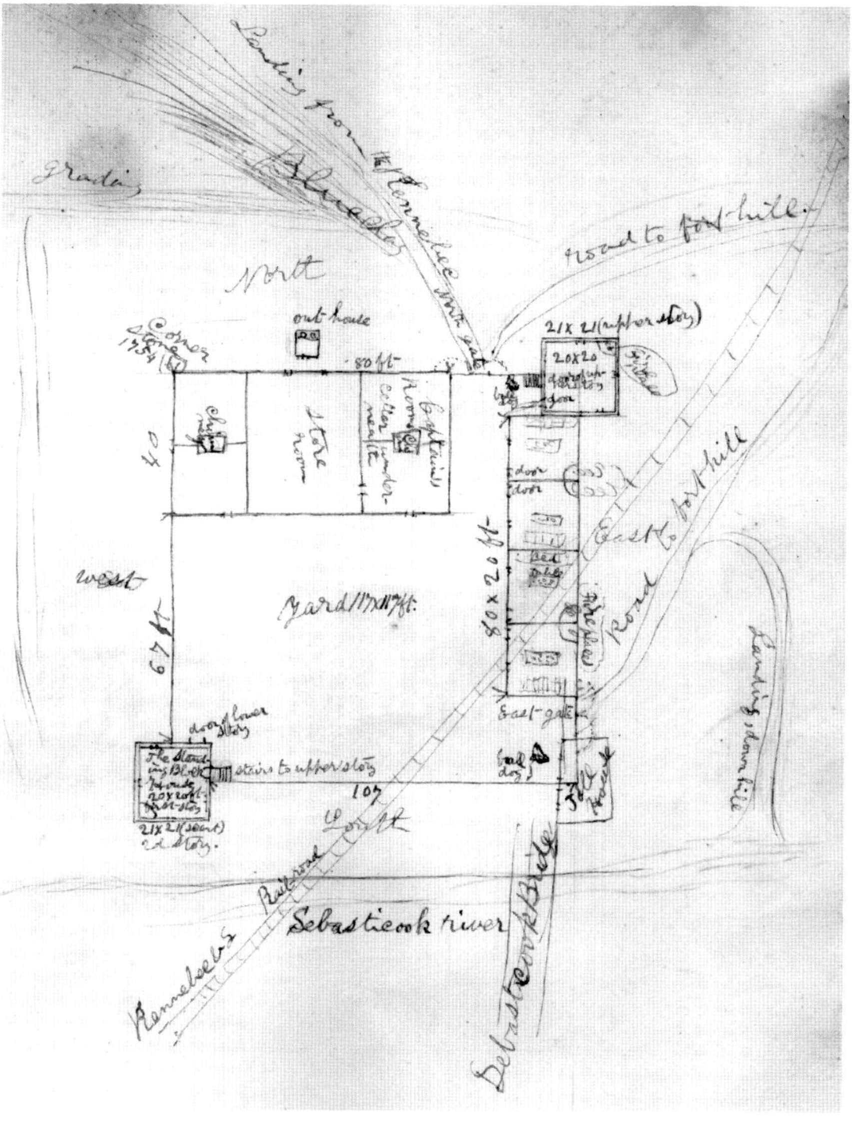

Sketch of the layout of Fort Halifax, by Timothy Paine, circa 1852. *Maine Historical Society*.

fort. These bullets were from friendly fire "[t]o see who should pay for the liquor." In fact, during his investigations in 1852, Paine caught a local man shooting at the blockhouse with a rifle.[135]

In the nineteenth century, the blockhouse had seen many uses: "Nathaniel Dingley, Senior, kept a store in the Old Block House—there were musters

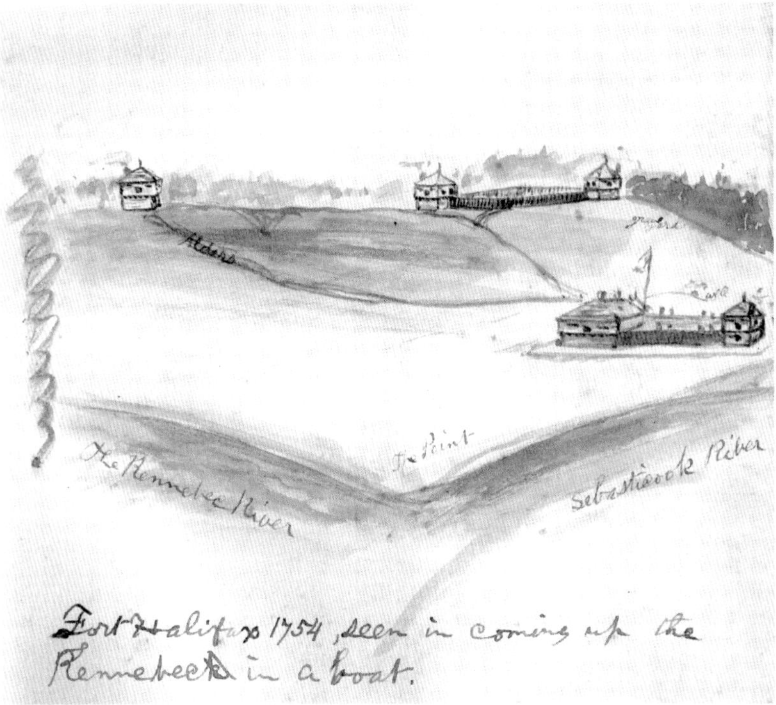

Sketch of Fort Halifax with three hill blockhouses, by Timothy Paine, circa 1852. *Maine Historical Society*.

Watercolor painting of Fort Halifax, from a grandfather clock owned by Thomas Rice of Winslow. *Winslow Public Library*.

on the Point then—it was used for a stable a few years ago, and lastly used for a hen-house." Paine offered an almost gothic-like description: "The spiderwebs are filled with dust and turned to cobwebs; there was a barn-swallow's nest in the roof, but a little mud only is left of it; there are wasps' nests in it, but they are empty; there is one dead hen mouldering among some dusty straw behind the stairs." While "the lock is gone from the door," it was "hasped to or stands open." Though the "inside is perfectly sound," the outside was not. The blockhouse listed "over cornerwise, towards the South west," and the "outside of the upper story is somewhat decayed, the South side very much so."[136] Later photos confirm that the upper story of the blockhouse was on the verge of collapse and show that the roof was in critical condition.

Despite the findings and detail of Paine's four articles in the *Eastern Mail*, his work caused little interest in the local area. The 100th anniversary of the construction of Fort Halifax in 1854–55 came and went, largely unnoticed by the Waterville-Winslow community. Hiram Simpson, tax collector, treasurer and constable of the town of Winslow, purchased several small lots

Fort Farm Point area, Winslow, circa 1859. *Winslow Historical Preservation Committee.*

on Fort Point from John Richards. One of these lots included the remaining blockhouse. The next year, he sold it to Asa Redington Jr. Town minutes and newspapers do not mention these sales; the town that had so needed the fort in order to establish itself had seemingly turned its back on its own history and heritage.[137] Citizens were likely preoccupied by the expansion of the railroad; in 1855, "the first train crossed into Waterville."[138]

The Winslow area was industrializing, and the blockhouse was a decayed vestige more suited for a landscape painting. Waterville-born businessman George F. Gilman had made a fortune in New York City in the leather-tanning business. He also started a coffee and tea company that became A&P Supermarkets. In 1863, he commissioned landscape painter James Hamilton Shegogue to paint the blockhouse. Shegogue completed and signed his painting in 1864. The blockhouse is elongated and looks less decayed than Paine's descriptions suggest. It seemed like Shegogue never visited the blockhouse but rather attempted to capture for Gilman, living in the bustle of Manhattan, what Gilman wanted to remember.[139]

Fort Halifax, by James Hamilton Shegogue, circa 1864. *Maine Historical Society.*

For many, Fort Halifax had little place in the transforming central Maine landscape. In 1865, workers carted off the stone foundation of the Fort House for use in building a nearby home. In 1867, a year after Elizabeth Freeman died, a reporter for the *Kennebec Journal* called the blockhouse a "dilapidated piece of furniture" and believed that the "printed pages of history will serve all the purposes of that crumbling, tiny little pen." An unknown *Waterville Mail* columnist disagreed. Rather, the unknown author continued, townspeople must take action in order to save the blockhouse before it was too late. "At a trifling cost [the blockhouse] might have been—indeed, it still might be preserved." The author lamented vandals' "stupidity." The blockhouse, instead of being cherished, had "been used alternatively as a boathouse, a store house for farm-tools, a cow-house and a hen-coup, [*sic*] and it is now, a correspondent informs us, in a tumble down and particularly disagreeable condition." Moreover, the author exclaimed, "there is a general indifference in relation to the preservation of interesting relics of the past."[140]

By the late 1860s and early 1870s, the remaining blockhouse of Fort Halifax had reached a critical point and was on the verge of complete collapse. As one distressed citizen noted in the *Waterville Mail*, "It seems that Fort Halifax, which is now standing but is being permitted to go to ruin, is one hundred and thirteen years old, and public measures ought to be inaugurated for its future preservation." Asa Redington Jr. sold the old blockhouse and the land around it to the Ticonic Water Power Company in 1867, but the company gave no guarantees of future preservation.[141]

Instead of preserving the fort, many people preferred to seize chunks of the old blockhouse. In 1871, as rail traffic in Maine increased, the first full train of Pullman Palace Cars to travel east of Boston passed by Fort Halifax on its way to Bangor. The train halted to let off passengers at a station located just a few hundred yards south of the blockhouse on the present-day Augusta Road. The tourists then "inspected [the] curious relic of antiquity."[142] The *Portland Daily Press* reported that "'[s]plinters' from this ancient fortification marked 'Fort Halifax 1754' will be found in many homes in Maine, New Hampshire, and Massachusetts, and a few more raids will accomplish what the Indians failed to do and that is, the reduction of the fort."[143]

By 1873, the voices of concerned citizens had prevailed, and a movement to preserve the fort took hold in both Winslow and Waterville. By 1873, Ticonic Water Power Company had leased the blockhouse to three local men—Dr. Atwood Crosby, Josiah W. Bassett and Albert Thomas "A.T." Shurtleff—"for the purpose of preservation." As an April 1873 edition of

Fort Halifax in disrepair, circa 1873. *Winslow Historical Preservation Committee.*

the *Waterville Mail* promised, "Immediate steps will be taken to fence and otherwise protect" the blockhouse.[144] Crosby had dropped out of Waterville College to serve in the Civil War and was, in 1873, a Waterville physician. Bassett, a local print master, was Winslow's town clerk and postmaster. Shurtleff was a farmer and an officer in the Maine militia. He lived with his brother and mother in the Gothic cottage on the Augusta Road.[145] The April 26, 1873 issue of the *Maine Farmer* hailed the trio as "patriotic citizens" and added that "[w]ithout such care," the blockhouse "would have fallen to pieces in a short time." Crosby, Bassett and Shurtleff quickly reconstructed the blockhouse with no known major setbacks.[146]

Accompanying this restoration was a renewed interest in the history of Fort Halifax and the region in general. Though it said little about the restoration process, the *Waterville Mail* printed weekly articles on the history of Fort Halifax from February 13, 1874, to March 27, 1874, spurring more public interest and local enthusiasm. Dr. Crosby also found the time to make a hatchet for himself. The *Maine Farmer* reported that "the handle [was] made of a bit of oak taken from the old blockhouse which once formed a part of the defenses of Fort Halifax."[147] Dr. Crosby was one of the few relic hunters who deserve pardon. An unsigned ad in the May 15, 1874 *Waterville Mail* proudly announced that the "old block house on Fort Point has been repaired and placed in condition to endure for another half century." The article then thanked Crosby, Bassett, Shurtleff and "all others who have interested themselves in preserving this relic of the olden time or aided the enterprise in any way."

Just as these restoration efforts took hold, ownership of the blockhouse again transferred hands. The Lockwood Company purchased all real

Renovated Fort Halifax blockhouse, circa 1874. *Stan Mathieu.*

Lithograph of Fort Halifax as it looked in 1756. *Stan Mathieu.*

estate and water rights from the Ticonic Water Power Company in 1875.[148] As interest in the fort reached beyond Winslow, artists, journalists and historians questioned the notion of a third blockhouse on the hill above Fort Halifax. An 1872 lithograph showed otherwise. Two years later, the *Waterville Mail* questioned Paine's assertion "that a third block house was erected after Montresor's visit," calling such a claim "wanting in probability." Two years later, historian William Goold concluded that "Mr. P is mistaken…there were but two, the larger one 34 x 34 the other 20 x 20." By the 1870s, it seemed widely known that there were only two blockhouses on the hill.[149]

Goold's conclusions were the product of his visit to Winslow the winter before. In December 1875, William Goold of Windham, Maine, visited the recently restored blockhouse. Goold was a retired tailor turned farmer and had recently served in the state senate. He was also a history buff and an active member of the Maine Historical Society. He researched the fort and prepared a sketch for the society based on his findings.[150] Eventually, Goold wrote "Fort Halifax: Its Projectors, Builders, and Garrison" and read it at the society's meeting in Portland on March 30, 1876. One might assume, Goold noted, that the final standing blockhouse of Fort Halifax "was simply a timber house or camp to hide in from the Indians, not supposing that it is

Sketch of Fort Halifax, by William Goold, 1876. *Maine Historical Society.*

less than one-tenth part of the buildings of the strongest and most extensive fortress in Maine" of the eighteenth century.[151]

Goold spoke for an hour and a half before the Maine Historical Society on Fort Halifax and the individuals and events that were directly connected with its history. He also revealed the trials and fears that the common soldiers faced while serving at Fort Halifax and discussed Fort Halifax's historical importance. The *Portland Daily Press* declared that "no abstract can do justice to Mr. Gold's interesting paper" on Fort Halifax.[152] To this day, his paper and his sketches offer a valuable resource to anyone who is interested in the history of Fort Halifax.

By 1879, the remaining blockhouse was in the care of the Maine Historical Society, and the society continued to collect items related to the fort.[153]

Relic hunters, too, raided the blockhouse and the site of the fort. They grabbed rare Native American artifacts and unearthed Indian skeletons. In 1884, perhaps in response to these raids, a "handsome sign" with the inscription "Fort Halifax; erected 1754" was placed on the old blockhouse by the Maine Central Railroad Company, which had taken over ownership. The placing of the sign was hailed as an example of "enlightened self-interest that promotes public good."[154]

A key to the Fort House at Fort Halifax. *Maine Historical Society.*

Despite the attentions of such men as Paine and Goold, much of the nineteenth century marked a time of neglect for Fort Halifax. Even after the 1873–74 restoration of the remaining blockhouse, relic hunters were out in full force, destroying the old blockhouse bit by bit. As Maine moved into the twentieth century, would the blockhouse be rescued by dedicated caregivers set on preserving it or would it find itself vandalized and chipped away by short-sighted relic hunters until there was nothing left? The 1873–74 restoration and local media coverage had rekindled historical interest in Fort Halifax, but this interest was, potentially, a double-edged sword.

Chapter 6

New Owners, New Nostalgia, 1890–1970

On April 24, 1897, the *Lewiston Evening Journal* described the fort site in rich detail: "Enclosed within a dilapidated picket fence through which the goldenrod and weeds push themselves in picturesque confusion, this old block house is all that remains of Fort Halifax."[155] In the last decade of the nineteenth century, the blockhouse was in poor shape. As a *Colby Echo* article had explained in 1893, "Everything about it shows the marks of neglect and ill-usage." Souvenir hunters had taken a heavy and noticeable toll on the old blockhouse: "Every available bit of wood has been carried off by enthusiastic visitors. Even the stairs, and parts of the heavy plank floor have gradually ceased to be."[156] Business traveler Charles A. Allen added, "You will notice by the photographs that there are many places in the timber which have been dug out with knives, and I was told that a great many bullets have been obtained in this way."[157]

While the blockhouse certainly remained a popular local destination at this time, its condition had also reached a deep low point. However, the turn of the century also saw renewed calls from the local community to preserve the landmark. "The blockhouse is said to be the last of its kind and period in New England," the *Colby Echo* reported. "If this is true, it certainly is to be hoped that some kind hand will rescue it from the knife of the relic-seeker, and secure its preservation before it becomes a thing of the past."[158]

The period between 1890 and 1970 served as a highly transformative era for the town of Winslow and, consequently, for Fort Halifax. As the Kennebec Valley modernized and industrialized, neglect and disinterest left a dilapidated and fast-decaying blockhouse. However, an appreciation for the past took hold of the people of Winslow and the region, gradually reinvigorating the fort's former prominence. Waterville's centennial, the Daughters of the American Revolution (DAR) and various local commemorations all helped to fuel this enthusiasm for the past. As a result, the blockhouse took on new meanings for the citizens of Winslow. The condition of the fort's remnant continued to reflect the town's economic and social trajectory. The ruins of Fort Halifax and the town of Winslow were deeply intertwined.

By the 1890s, central Maine was industrializing at a rapid pace. Manufacturing had transformed Winslow economically and demographically. The Hollingsworth and Whitney Pulp and Paper Company (later Scott Paper), built a massive plant upriver on the Kennebec in 1892. Proctor & Bowie Company opened its sawmill, brickyard and lumber supply facility in 1898. Fort Point, at the confluence of the Kennebec and the Sebasticook Rivers, also transformed. The Lockwood Company owned land on the point from 1875 to 1902. Its owner, William T. Reynolds, built and operated a large sawmill there. For eight months of the year, it employed sixty-five workers, who produced shingles sold in Boston. And the company that became Central Maine Power constructed an electric power generation station on the Sebasticook in 1899. Manufacturing jobs brought hundreds of Scottish, French Canadian and Polish immigrant families to Winslow. In 1880, Winslow's population was 1,467. By 1920, it was 3,300.[159]

The blockhouse on the Sebasticook sat in the shadow of industrializing Winslow. But with this development and the faster pace of life that accompanied it, interest in the blockhouse waned. Bangor attorney Albert Ware Paine, eighty-eight, at the time Colby's oldest living alumnus, published a poem on Fort Halifax found in the papers of his late brother Timothy in the *Bangor Daily Commercial* in 1900 in an attempt to keep the fort in the public consciousness.[160]

Albert Paine's wishes were realized. In the summer of 1902, the Lockwood Company sold the blockhouse to the Maine Central Railroad. Judge Charles F. Johnson, born in Winslow in 1859, oversaw the transfer of ownership. He understood the historical importance of the blockhouse and included in the deed a requirement that all subsequent owners must preserve and repair the blockhouse as best as realistically possible.[161] Events in the winter of 1905 almost prevented this. Two sections of a freight train crashed on the bridge passing by the blockhouse, setting alight six railroad cars.[162] Townspeople, the railroad and the fire department rushed into action. Using snow to extinguish the fire, townspeople, railroad workers and firemen contained the flames and saved the blockhouse.

This image, dated September 1896, shows mill buildings behind the blockhouse. *Stan Mathieu.*

View of Fort Halifax from a postcard, circa 1900. *Winslow Historical Preservation Committee.*

Old Fort Halifax, taken from an electric car, September 1913, by James B. Small of Lyme, Maine. *Maine Historical Society.*

The year 1913 signaled a new era for Fort Halifax's blockhouse. On March 17, 1913, two Winslow women—Carrie Stratton Howard and Minnie Garland—formed a new chapter of the Daughters of the American Revolution. Howard, Timothy Paine's great-niece, became the chapter's first regent. Her husband, Horace, suggested naming the chapter after Fort Halifax and made a gavel from a piece of wood taken from the blockhouse. Garland's great-grandfather, Ralph Farnham, was the last known American survivor of the Battle of Bunker Hill and died in Acton, Maine, at age 104. Carrie Howard and Garland "got the Rail road (Maine Central) to put a [flag] pole up at the fort." On July 4, 1913, they held a ceremony at the blockhouse. Civil War veteran Ambrose Merrow, father of chapter member Sadie Tukey, hoisted the American flag over the fort for the first time. For the next fifty years, the DAR flew an American flag over the blockhouse.[163] While Winslow seemed apathetic about the fort in the 1890s and early 1900s, mindsets changed with the founding of the Fort Halifax chapter of the DAR, a group dedicated to appreciating and preserving American history and historical sites.

The following year, Colby College students showed their enduring interest in the fort. For years, Colby art students had journeyed to Fort Point and had painted the blockhouse. Now, the newly formed Colby Outing Club visited Fort Halifax on its way to tour the Winslow tin mine. And two years later, students from the Good Will-Hinckley School in the nearby town of

Good Will boys at Fort Halifax, Winslow, 1916. *L.C. Bates Museum/Maine Memory Network.*

Fairfield took a field trip to the blockhouse and posed for photos. In the mid-twentieth century, the fort became an oasis for young people growing up in a fast-changing world.[164]

The year 1921 marked the 150th anniversary of the founding of Winslow. The DAR planned and led ceremonies and a parade, which took place the day after a devastating tornado. Jennie Paine Howard of the Fort Halifax Chapter, also the head librarian at Winslow Public Library, delivered a lively reading of the town's history. Though immigration and industry had transformed the landscape of the core of the town, she waxed nostalgic: "Winslow always has been and is thoroughly American…the town is typical of America…The town today at heart is what she was a hundred or even a hundred and fifty years ago."[165] Howard's words exemplify the historical enthusiasm and new nostalgia that the DAR inspired. Like it did to Timothy Paine and to the citizens of the nineteenth century, the blockhouse also captured the attention of Alexander Baird, a Winslow High School student and member of the class of 1922. He penned a poem, "Fort Halifax," for the school's *Periscope* literary magazine.[166] While it selectively celebrated the past at a time of economic and social change, the sesquicentennial helped to transform attitudes and soon brought changes for the blockhouse.

A view of the blockhouse from Lithgow Street, circa 1920. *Winslow Town Office Building.*

Somehow Fort Halifax remained in the town's consciousness. Of the dozens of new businesses and civic organizations established in the twentieth century, many included Fort Halifax in their title and would continue to do so, testifying to the enduring influence of the fort on Winslow's identity. The Fort Halifax Power Company, several Masonic organizations, a band, a bowling team, Fort Halifax Inn, Fort Halifax Gas and Fuel and the Fort Halifax Packing Company derived their names from Winslow's historic outpost.

In the 1920s, the DAR also took a momentous step in the preservation of Fort Halifax. When "some people in Waterville started talking of moving it across the river," chapter historian Mary Howard recalled, Carrie Stratton Howard and Minnie Garland made several trips to Portland and wrote numerous letters. Their efforts paid off—the Maine Central Railroad deeded the blockhouse to the chapter on May 26, 1924.[167] The ladies commemorated this event on June 2 with an elaborate celebration. Notable Winslow residents, descendants of the fort's builders and soldiers and politicians attended. Maine state representative William Tudor Gardiner, great-great-great-grandson of Dr. Silvester Gardiner, was there. So was Maine governor Percival Baxter. "We are living in an age of speed," Baxter declared to the crowd, "and we do not take time to think, but on this historic spot we are to take the time to look back and think of the sacrifices and hardships that were made by our ancestors."[168] Winslow and much of Maine were caught up in the frenzy of

Aerial photo of Fort Point, circa 1950s. *Morning Sentinel.*

modernization and industrialization, yet Baxter and the DAR represented a growing counter trend. The governor campaigned hard for the protection of natural and historic places. He saved and protected a total of eight forts in Maine. The ceremony culminated with the placing of a tablet on the outside wall of the old blockhouse to commemorate the transfer of the deed. Soon after, the chapter raised state and local funds and purchased a building close to the fort that many saw as a fire risk.[169]

From the 1930s to the 1950s, Winslow's landmark was overshadowed and impinged, yet efforts to save and document the blockhouse continued. A construction firm sat on the point. So did a railroad spur leading to Winslow Coal Company. Texaco oil and gas tanks were perched close to the Sebasticook, just west of the blockhouse. By the mid-1940s, Capital Distributors' warehouse and Norman Woodbury's used car lot also occupied the land.[170]

Fort Halifax Chapter, DAR, made intermittent "necessary repairs and replacements to the blockhouse." But floods inflicted damage and expense. In late March 1936, the *Waterville Morning Sentinel* reported,

A collector's plate made in Germany, early 1900s. *Winslow Public Library.*

"Workmen toiled frantically to check the rapid surge of ice and water by means of bags of sand and car loads of rock." The blockhouse survived with just water damage to some of its walls. The DAR replaced the roof and a few rotted-out lower timbers and built a new fence. These fixes were noted by representatives from the Historic American Buildings Survey later that year. A federal program created to employ architects and draftsmen during the Great Depression, the survey's workers documented the blockhouse in great detail. Little did they know their work would one day prove indispensable.[171]

Not only was the blockhouse neglected and endangered by flooding, but also it was largely inaccessible. Capital Distributors allegedly blocked access to the point.[172] Immigrant and ethnic divisions in Winslow limited what

Floodwaters, March 1936. *Winslow Public Library.*

children could enjoy the fort. In 2013, two retirees recalled these divides. Stan Mathieu grew up in a French Canadian family in south Winslow. He often played in and around the blockhouse. But Jack Nivison, who was about the same age but came from a Scottish immigrant family, rarely ventured from his home in north Winslow to the French-dominated south Winslow for fear of being bullied. Everyone did not share Fort Halifax equally.[173]

Lack of funds limited the DAR's ability to make any larger restorations, but it held bridge tournaments, yard sales and other fundraisers to maintain the blockhouse. In 1948, the chapter received award money from the National DAR for its service and dedication, which went toward a new sign. In 1953, the blockhouse again withstood a flood, undoing some of the DAR's efforts.[174]

The year 1954 marked the 200th anniversary of the construction of Fort Halifax. On July 20, 250 people, plus television crews, gathered for the Maine DAR Field Day, hosted by Regent Hope Wixson and the Fort Halifax chapter. Active in the local grange, Wixson lived on Garland Road with her husband, Eldwin, an insurance salesman and dairy farmer. She was a writer for the *Waterville Morning Sentinel*. Three of the chapter's charter members dressed in period costume. The Maine DAR donated a plaque to the chapter. The 1954 ceremony showed the ever-changing significance of the blockhouse. Local dignitaries delivered impassioned speeches in which

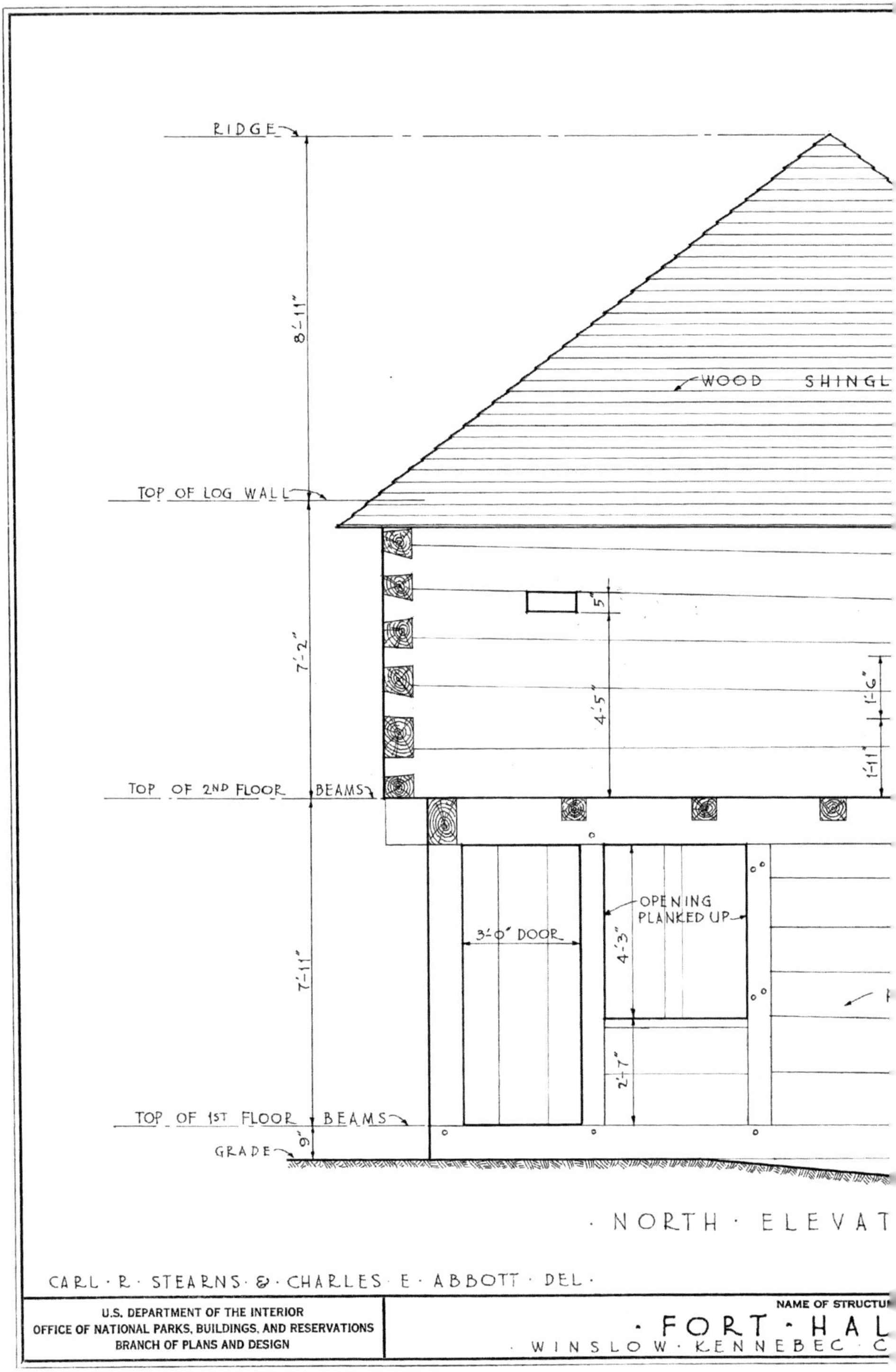
RIDGE
8'-11"
WOOD SHINGL
TOP OF LOG WALL
7'-2"
5"
4'-5"
1'-6"
1'-11"
TOP OF 2ND FLOOR BEAMS
OPENING PLANKED UP
3'-0" DOOR
4'-3"
7'-11"
2'-7"
TOP OF 1ST FLOOR BEAMS
9"
GRADE
· NORTH · ELEVAT
CARL · R · STEARNS · & · CHARLES · E · ABBOTT · DEL ·
U.S. DEPARTMENT OF THE INTERIOR
OFFICE OF NATIONAL PARKS, BUILDINGS, AND RESERVATIONS
BRANCH OF PLANS AND DESIGN
NAME OF STRUCTU
· FORT · HAL
· WINSLOW · KENNEBEC · C

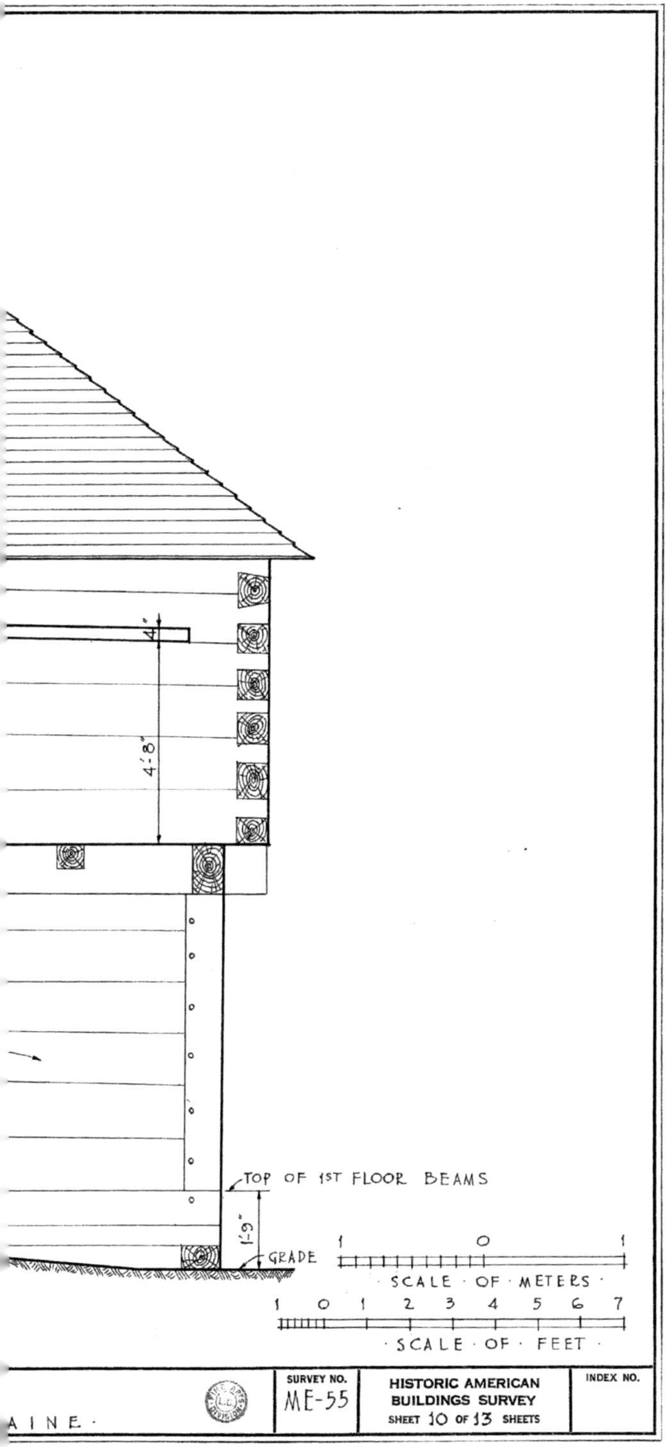

Architectural drawing of the Fort Halifax blockhouse, by the Historic American Buildings Survey, 1936. *Library of Congress.*

Above: Image from an Eastern Illustrating Company negative, 1951. *Penobscot Marine Museum*.

Left: Bea White, Priscilla McKallip and Grace Towle prepare the blockhouse for the Maine DAR Field Day, July 11, 1954. *Fort Halifax Chapter, DAR*.

they marshaled the fort as a symbol for the anti-communist movement amid fears of nuclear war with the Soviet Union. Colonel Raymond Rogers, a Waterville attorney, spoke on "Americanism." Waterville attorney Thomas N. Weeks—who had secured the deed for the blockhouse in 1924—urged people to rally against "subversive ideological theories." Overlooking the colonization of Indian lands two hundred years earlier, he considered the fort a symbol of "our continued resistance to invasions by all foreign themes and theories." U.S. representative Charlie Nelson, recalled to Washington at the last minute, wrote that "[d]eath by atoms today can hold no more terror for us than did death by tomahawk and knife for our ancestors."[175]

During this time, the landscape surrounding the blockhouse changed as well. In June 1956, the Maine Central Railroad donated and installed a new flag pole. DAR member Charlotte Norton hoisted the flag in a ceremony on June 13. Don and Francelia Corbett, owners of Fort Halifax Packing Company, donated funds for preservation.[176]

Further, construction crews finished a new four-lane bridge across the Sebasticook in the spring of 1960. Hope Wixson convinced her colleagues at the *Waterville Morning Sentinel* to dub the bridge the "Fort Halifax Bridge." Maine's legislature and governor followed suit, passing a resolve on February 15, 1961, to the same effect.[177]

With this new bridge came state plans for the development of the Arnold Trail Historic Pilgrimage Trail. In 1962, two state representatives met with Wixson and several DAR members and inspected the blockhouse. They were Ambrose Cramer, a historic preservation expert and architect from Rockland, and Clyde Manwell of Maine State Parks. Cramer saw the pressing need to use a concrete foundation to prevent against the threat of floods but otherwise happily reported on the "wonderful state of preservation." He recognized the historical and recreational potential of the adjacent area. He hoped that it might become the centerpiece of a more visitor-friendly public space. At present, he determined, the blockhouse was "A PRICELESS GEM in a mediocre setting."[178] Despite this assessment, visitors kept coming; in 1964, the Colby College Outing Club again visited the blockhouse, this time to celebrate its fiftieth anniversary.[179]

In October 1965, the blockhouse again changed hands. The Maine state government could provide a steady source of funding toward historical preservation that the DAR's best efforts could not match. Therefore, the DAR relinquished ownership to the state. A small ceremony commemorated this transfer. Minnie Garland, ninety-two, a charter

DAR ladies and local dignitaries gather after the 1954 ceremony. *Fort Halifax Chapter, DAR.*

Area youth observe the 1956 flagpole dedication ceremony. *Fort Halifax Chapter, DAR.*

Clyde Manwell, Ethel Lancaster, Shirley Witham and Ambrose Cramer meet at the blockhouse, August 1962. *Hope Wixson DAR Papers, Winslow Public Library.*

Minnie Garland hands the deed to Charles Bradford, October 29, 1965. *Fort Halifax Chapter, DAR.*

member of the Fort Halifax chapter in 1913, handed the deed to a state parks official, Charles Bradford. Juanita Peters lowered the American flag. Bradford hoisted the flag of the state of Maine.[180] The deed was officially recorded as transferred on January 19, 1966. The town secured additional land on Fort Point from Bill's Oil Service in 1967 for just one dollar. Maine Historic Preservation Commission efforts paid dividends. In 1968, Fort Halifax became a National Historic Landmark and joined the National Register of Historic Places.[181]

To meet its changing needs, Winslow replaced its town meeting and selectman form of government with a town council and town manager in 1969. By 1970, the population of Winslow had reached 9,800 people, several times its number during the nineteenth century. On the outskirts of town, thriving dairy and poultry farms fed New England.[182]

The blockhouse, meanwhile, was in the hands of the state, and the surrounding property on Fort Point was in disarray. The basement of Capitol Distributors' warehouse on Fort Point overlapped the foundation of Lithgow's fort. The used car lot of Woodbury Motor Company, too, sat on Fort Point, and its office piazza lay on top of one of the fort's wells. The blockhouse was dilapidated, and its roof again needed repair. Few residents journeyed there, save for children playing or the occasional tourist. Even more disturbing was talk that Fort Point might become the site of a sewage treatment plant. What would come of Ambrose Cramer's enthusiasm for the historical and recreational potential of the adjacent area?[183]

Chapter 7

Creating Fort Halifax Park, 1970–1987

In 1970, Pearley Lachance, president of the Winslow Historical Society, pitched an idea to the town council after researching land deeds and reflecting on the significance of the site: to build a park on Fort Point. In the early 1970s, several forces coalesced to raise interest in preserving Fort Point and the blockhouse. The Maine Historic Preservation Commission and the Winslow Town Council endorsed the idea. There had been talk to build a sewage treatment plant on Fort Point. The blockhouse had recently become a National Historic Landmark. A 1972 booklet by Colonel Carleton Fisher of the Maine National Guard attracted interest in the early history of the fort. The 200th anniversary of Winslow's founding, Arnold's Expedition and American independence rekindled historical awareness. National trends also played a role. The passage of the Clean Water Act of 1972 and other federal environmental legislation began a cleanup of Maine's rivers. Now, people considered the recreational value of the Kennebec and Sebasticook. But converting the dense brush, used car lot and warehouses near the blockhouse into a park would not be easy.[184]

A few years went by. Steve Clark, a Winslow resident and a teacher at the Regional Vocational Center in Waterville, took action when he learned of the possibility of a sewage plant being built in the shadow of Fort Halifax. Writing on behalf of the Winslow Conservation Commission in June 1974, Clark provided the vision for a park. He called for landscape enhancement, walking trails, waterfront and boat access, better views of the rivers and a more developed historical exhibit. Many in Winslow

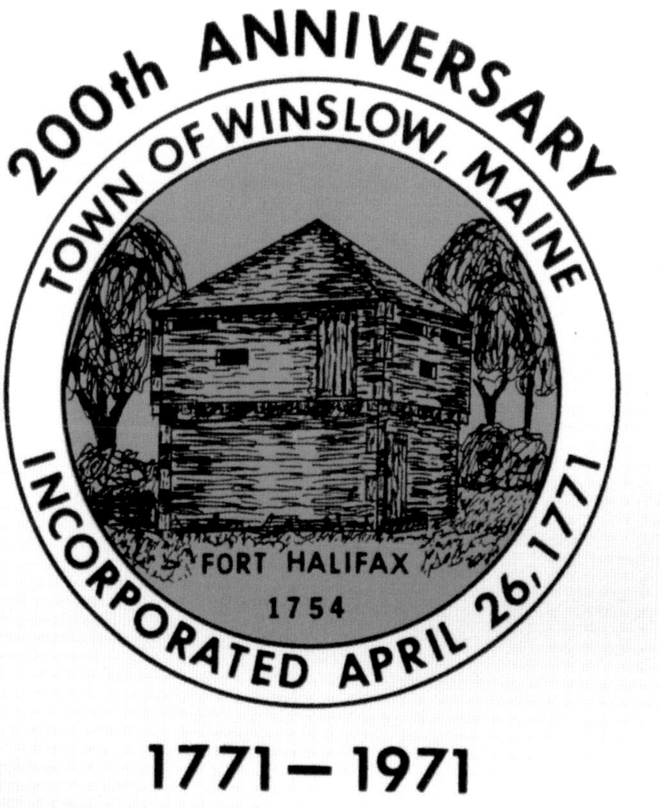

Commemorative tile made for the Winslow bicentennial, 1971. *Winslow Public Library.*

agreed. By the end of the year, the town council had authorized the purchase of two parcels of land on Fort Point—just over five acres owned by Woodbury Motor Company and half an acre consisting of a warehouse owned by Capital Distributors. It also set aside funds for park planning.[185]

The year 1975 marked a major and historic event in the fort's history and proved a consequential one for the blockhouse's future. In the fall of 1775, Benedict Arnold had traveled up the Kennebec and Chaudière Rivers to invade Quebec. His men had camped at and near Fort Halifax. Two hundred years later, six hundred volunteer reenactors retraced Arnold's footsteps.[186] The enthusiasm for these events rekindled interest in Fort Halifax.

The spotlight shone again on the blockhouse when the reenactment reached Waterville and Winslow. On a rainy Sunday, September 28,

Commemorative button made for the 1975 Arnold Expedition bicentennial, formerly owned by Leo Trahan. *Winslow Public Library*.

reenactment forces arrived by river, carried by bateaux. Rain dampened the gunpowder but did not stymie enthusiasm for this event. Colonel Thorton McGlamery, who portrayed Arnold during the bicentennial, exclaimed, "Rain! That's all part of it. There's a helluva lot of things worse than Rain!"[187] The reenactors met a second contingent of uniformed men who had traveled by foot. They were dressed in period clothing, some in buckskins and some in uniforms and carrying rifles, muskets and pistols. At Fort Point, Arnold's men demonstrated musket volleys and bateaux paddling techniques to hundreds of spectators. One observer noted that "an upstream current caused momentary unsteadiness as the boats were launched, but the men soon righted their craft with a practiced hand and rowed steadily to the landing opposite." After religious services, the men then moved on to set up camp at Winslow High School.[188]

Sunday the soldiers paraded through the town. Festivities continued in adjacent Waterville.[189] The march ended at the Civil War monument adjacent to Waterville's downtown area, and the troops staged a mock Revolutionary War skirmish. Local events ended that night, but the expedition continued up the Kennebec. Eventually, the participants traveled up the Chaudière River Valley to Quebec. There they restaged the December 31, 1775 battle, as Arnold and his men attempted to storm the walls of Quebec City.[190]

The Arnold bicentennial reinvigorated the historical spirit of Winslow. With media attention focused directly on Fort Halifax, the need to establish a historical recreational space around the blockhouse grew more urgent. As Ernie Baker of Winslow's Bicentennial Commission wrote in 1976, "It was felt by all members present that the area could be enjoyed by present and future Winslow citizens who would like a quiet place to relax in the heart of the town."[191] In the spring of 1976, the town secured state and federal matching grants to purchase the property on Fort Point. Before the end of the year, Norman Woodbury—gently nudged by his neighbor Steve Clark—sold the land occupied by his used car lot at a low price.[192] In the summer of 1977, the Maine Bureau of Parks and Recreation repaired the blockhouse. Using federal funds, the state replaced the roof, installed new foundation sills and installed a stair railing and a floor inside the blockhouse.[193]

But there was still no park on the point. Negotiations with Capital Distributors stalled, the result of lingering tensions from the dispute three decades earlier over access to the point through a right of way. Now, Capital also claimed that it needed the warehouse to store bottle returns. Neither party could agree on a suitable price. Owner Peter Calzolari and his attorney asked for $41,000, more than the property's assessed value. Finally, in June 1979, Calzolari sold the warehouse to Norman G. Poulin and Lee Spaulding of Pine Tree Furniture for $18,600. Pine Tree was unaware that Winslow eyed the property.[194]

One reporter surveyed the scene at Fort Point around the blockhouse: "Repeated floods [had] scattered wood and debris on the land and bushes and grass grew uncontrollably."[195] All this soon changed. On September 5, 1979, Leo Trahan of Winslow and Arthur Grenier of Waterville, both members of MacCrillis-Rousseau Veterans of Foreign Wars (VFW) Post 8835 in Winslow, announced big plans. They proposed "to provide picnic facilities on the grounds," to build a nature trail, a boat dock and "seaplane passenger facilities." Sam Boutin built a model of the original fort.[196] On the last weekend in September, various civic groups hosted a steamed-clam supper, a dance, a Catholic Mass, an open house at the VFW and militia demonstrations to mark the 225th anniversary of the building of Fort Halifax. Speaking in the drizzle to a small crowd assembled at the blockhouse, Grenier summed up the mission of those gathered: "We come here today to dedicate ourselves to the further development of the historic site." Energized participants formed a committee called the Friends of Fort Halifax. They built a coalition of local organizations, raised funds and worked with the town to finally create a park in the shadow of the Fort Halifax blockhouse.[197]

As interest increased, Parks and Recreation director Lee Breton and town manager Ed Gagnon secured grants from the state and federal government. Grenier spent the winter of 1979–80 writing letters. The Winslow Lions, Winslow Senior Citizens, local Boy Scouts, Knights of Columbus, firefighters and other civic organizations and individuals donated $5,600. During the summers of 1980 and 1981, they contributed countless hours of backbreaking labor as a massive cleanup effort began.[198] Students from the Waterville Regional Vocational Center built picnic tables and a gazebo. During the summers of 1981 through 1983, disadvantaged students, paid with federal funds, worked for minimum wage under the direction of schoolteacher Jack Nivison. They cleared the point of brush and debris. "It was like hacking through the Isthmus of Panama," Nivison recalled. Fire

Doug Fisher and Allen Jagger clean up Fort Point, 1981. *Morning Sentinel.*

Fort Halifax Days, by Dick Maxwell, August 1981. *Morning Sentinel.*

department crews burned the brush. Winslow Public Works graded the land and planted grass and trees. A park slowly took shape.[199]

With the blockhouse its most visible feature, on August 29, 1981, Fort Halifax Park opened with a ribbon-cutting ceremony. "Throughout the weekend, military bands played, speeches were given, and various civic and fraternal groups participated in the festivities": a two-day flea market and antiques fair, with games and activities, exhibits, food and drink.[200] By 1982, the citizens of Winslow had raised over $10,000 to augment a massive influx of state and federal funds.[201]

In 1983, Pine Tree Furniture, appreciating the beauty and potential of Fort Halifax Park, was more than willing to sell its warehouse. The town purchased the property at its appraised value—more than double the sum it had paid Capital—and Pine Tree found a new facility nearby.[202] In 1984, demolition crews took down the warehouse. In 1985 and 1986, local organizations donated and added more trees.[203]

No one was more surprised at the transformation than Pearley Lachance. In 1986, Lachance returned to Winslow after working in Algeria for more

Demolition Day, by Dick Maxwell, March 20, 1984. *Morning Sentinel.*

than a decade. The blockhouse and the land surrounding it only distantly resembled the dilapidated and neglected ruins that had existed a few decades earlier. A beautiful park, the collective effort of the entire town, stood in its place. In five years, townspeople had cleared dense vegetation, planted grass and hedges, built a gazebo and picnic tables and added grills. As Parks and Recreation director Lee Breton, who had been so vital to the efforts, wrote, Winslow residents had come together to transform "nothing more than a conglomeration of wood, auto parts, and other debris" into "what some individuals describe as one of the nicest parks in the state."[204] While Winslow had transformed economically and demographically, an enduring appreciation for the past had reemerged at intervals. In a venture that spanned nearly fifteen years, townspeople had come together to create a new future for the site of Fort Halifax and its remaining blockhouse.

Chapter 8

The Flood of 1987 and the Rebuilding Project, 1987–1989

On April 1, 1987, Jack Nivison, a teacher at Winslow High School, walked to work as he did almost every day. When he arrived, a custodian turned him around, informing him that school was closed that day due to flooded roads and bridges. Was this an April Fools' Day joke, Nivison wondered? With some persuasion, he returned home. He and his wife, Jo Ann, grabbed a camera and walked to Fort Point to see for themselves. A large snowpack, unusually high temperatures of fifty to sixty degrees and six to seven inches of rain had combined to bring a record-setting spring freshet to Maine. The flood soon garnered the nickname the "April Fools' Day Flood" and prompted Governor John R. McKernan Jr. to declare a state of emergency. As he and his wife viewed the rising waters, Nivison snapped a few photographs.[205]

The next day, roads and bridges were flooded or damaged. Work was cancelled for many people in Winslow and Waterville. So the Nivisons again scooped up their camera and walked toward Fort Halifax Park. They were unprepared for what they saw. Eight- to ten-foot-high floodwaters had inundated the low-lying land at the confluence of the Sebasticook and the Kennebec. Across the Sebasticook, houses had been lifted off their foundations on Lithgow Street. The Fort School and the Winslow Public Library were damaged. Fort Halifax Park was almost completely immersed. From almost the same vantage point as the previous day, the Nivisons again chronicled the devastation. Where the blockhouse had previously stood, they saw nothing but floodwater. The torrent had swept the Fort Halifax

View of Fort Halifax Park, April 1, 1987. *Jack Nivison.*

One of the last photos of Fort Halifax, by Dick Maxwell, April 1, 1987. *Morning Sentinel.*

View of Fort Halifax, April 2, 1987. *Jack Nivison.*

A view from the air, by Dick Maxwell, April 2, 1987. *Morning Sentinel.*

A view from Lithgow Street, showing where the blockhouse once stood, May 1987. *Jack Nivison.*

blockhouse, the iconic symbol of a community, down the Kennebec in the middle of the night. No one saw it disappear.[206] As Gerry Boyle of the *Central Maine Morning Sentinel* quipped, "It had survived the French and Indian War, marauding bands of hostile Indians and years of neglect. But the Fort Halifax blockhouse, built in 1754, could not withstand the torrent of the flood of 1987."[207]

Almost immediately, the state began a frantic search for the pieces of Winslow's lost historic gem. State authorities received dozens of reports of the missing blockhouse from people along the Kennebec. One resident in Sidney claimed to have seen the entire fort "lashed to a tree." Another person in Augusta reported that it was pinned against a railroad bridge. Both reports turned out to be false, though a portion of the 1977 restored roof turned up under the old Richmond-Dresden Bridge in 2013.[208] The Maine Bureau of Parks and Recreation and the Department of Inland Fisheries and Wildlife sent planes to search up and down the river for the blockhouse, but to no avail. By April 10, various state agencies confirmed that the blockhouse had broken into individual logs and traveled down the Kennebec.[209]

Workers recover blockhouse timbers from the Kennebec, April 1987. *Stan Mathieu.*

Blockhouse timbers loaded for transport to Winslow Public Works, April 1987. *Stan Mathieu.*

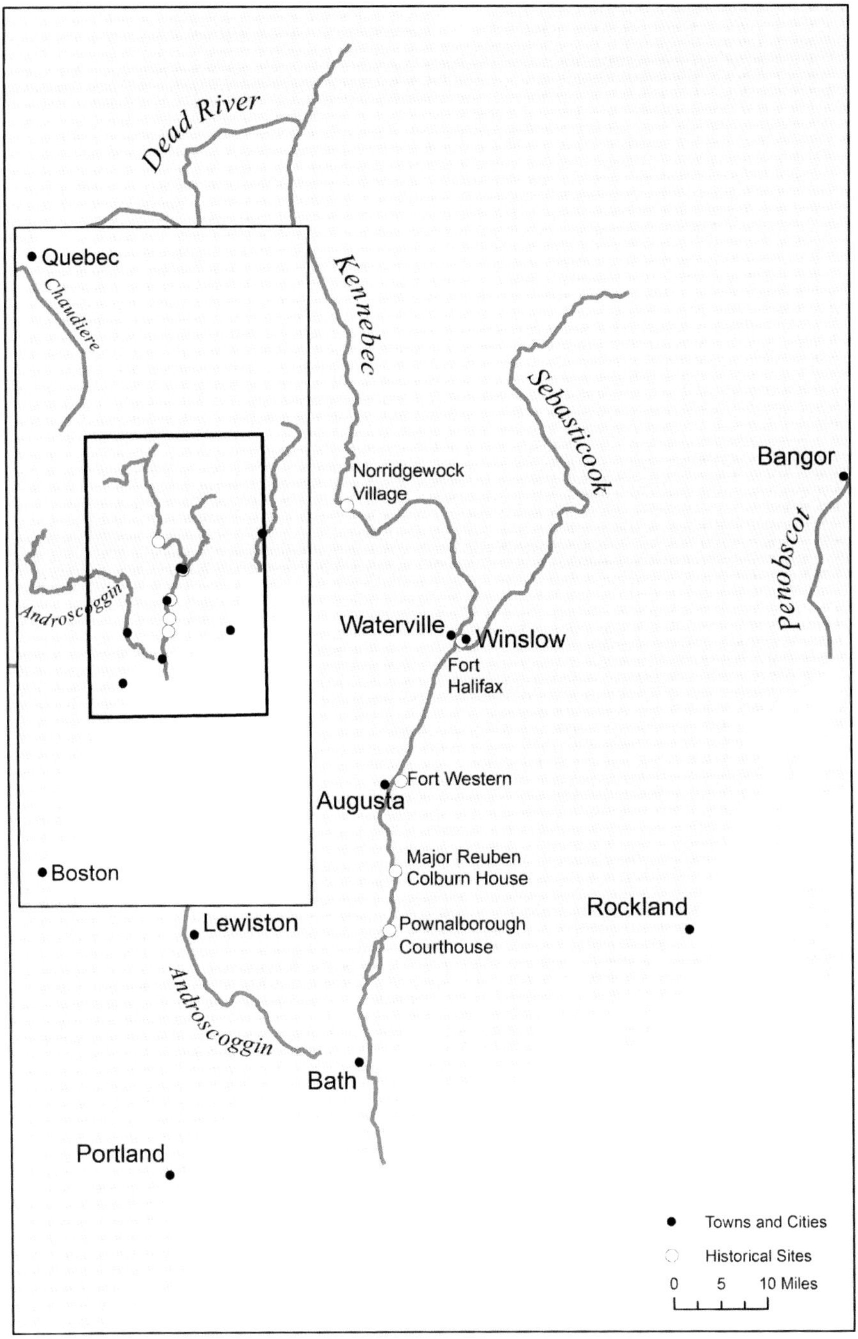

Fort Halifax in the modern era. *Manny Gimond.*

Throughout May, June and July, timbers from the old blockhouse washed up on beaches and islands in the lower Kennebec. Much of the second floor turned up just north of Bath at Day's Ferry. Campers on Whaleboat Island in Casco Bay spotted a curious old log in early July. Another camper spotted a piece of metal laying facedown. He picked it up thinking "it would be ideal for a planned clambake."[210] On the opposite side, he discovered an inscription commemorating Fort Halifax on its 200th anniversary in 1954. The search for the scattered wreckage of Fort Halifax concluded that summer. Old logs were stored at Winslow's Public Works Department while the state and the town began pondering the next series of actions. Thirty-three original wall timbers were found.[211]

With this dramatic and tragic event, Winslow citizens reflected on Fort Halifax's significance. Throughout its existence, it had served as a political, social and economic center of the town. As they had in years past, Winslow residents and the local area sprang into action. Three days after the blockhouse's disappearance, the *Central Maine Morning Sentinel* lent its support. It raised $12,500 by issuing a "Souvenir Edition" covering the flood. A new Friends of Fort Halifax organization took the lead. By August, it had incorporated as a nonprofit organization and raised funds. It rallied individuals, civic organizations, town government and state and federal officials to the cause. State representative Donald V. Carter, president of the Friends, used his connections in Augusta and Washington, D.C., to push through government action. He even tried, unsuccessfully, to get a postage stamp made. The Friends later learned that the State of Maine had flood insurance on the blockhouse, which was a huge relief.[212]

State representative Donald V. Carter, circa 1987. *Winslow Town Office Building.*

As the state collected timbers from the Kennebec, discussion concerning the restoration began immediately. Most Winslow citizens never debated whether to rebuild the blockhouse.

However, townspeople heavily discussed how and to what extent the fort should be rebuilt. In the earliest stages of brainstorming, some residents, particularly the Friends of Fort Halifax, favored a proposal to restore the fort to its former glory. They wished to rebuild the entire fort, including the old palisade wall and the other buildings.[213] Other plans suggested a phantom structure, with markers outlining the location of other buildings. In light of the sudden, tragic disappearance of the last vestige of Fort Halifax, the Winslow community grew resolved and optimistic. Peter Blais of the *Central Maine Morning Sentinel* wrote, "The storm clouds that washed away the Fort Halifax blockhouse this spring may have had a silver lining that could lead to the restoration of almost the entire fort."[214]

However, before any restoration effort could begin, this site of historic and prehistoric significance required an archaeological excavation. Lee Cranmer, an archaeologist with the Maine Historic Preservation Commission, hoped to discover the exact and original location of the fort. He wondered if the railroad company had moved the blockhouse in the 1840s.[215] From August 17 to August 28, 1987, Cranmer and Anne Hilton, another Maine archaeologist, excavated an area six feet by twenty feet. They confirmed

Archaeologists at work, by Dick Maxwell, August 1987. *Morning Sentinel.*

the location of the original blockhouse. The team uncovered a posthole forty-one inches deep, which Cranmer suspected was the roof support of the blockhouse. In addition, they found numerous remnants of Indian fire pits and pottery. They submitted stone tools and charcoal they found for radiocarbon dating. Results confirmed that Native Americans had been at the site over 3,200 years ago, but Cranmer believed that Indians were in the area 7,000 years ago.[216]

In May and again in August 1988, Cranmer and Art Speiss of the Maine Historic Preservation Commission returned to the site of Fort Halifax. Cranmer's crew dug four holes six inches deep and spaced a few feet apart "in hopes of covering a big enough area that you'll eventually come across something," he told the *Sentinel*. They made several exciting discoveries. The posthole found in 1987 had actually served as the corner of a temporary palisade that preceded the blockhouse during the initial construction. "They were in a hurry to build a wall around themselves because they were afraid of being attacked." In the May dig, a twelve-year-old boy, "complete with

Joan Robertson of Litchfield sorting findings, by Ron Maxwell, May 1988. *Morning Sentinel.*

crewcut and high-top sneakers," found a piece of Indian pottery estimated at 3,000 to 3,200 years old.[217]

The fantastic success of this archaeology and the thousands of items recovered—knives, forks, ceramics, buttons, pipes, nails, glass and Indian artifacts—demonstrated the immense historic and prehistoric significance of the peninsula and reminded people that that the soldiers who built Fort Halifax and the settlers who created the town of Winslow shared the same earth with thousands of years of Native American civilization.

Through the fall and winter of 1987 and 1988, the State of Maine received bids for the restoration project from several contractors. In early 1988, the state selected the bid and proposal of Stan Mathieu of Winslow. Mathieu's bid came in at $89,650, well under the $96,000 it had collected from flood insurance.[218] As Elliot Potter of the *Central Maine Morning Sentinel* wrote, "The fort has been a landmark, a recurring part of his life, as it has for so many other natives and residents of this area."[219] Mathieu had played at the blockhouse when he was a child. He graduated from Colby College, joined the U.S. Air Force and then studied both Fort Halifax and the *Waterville Morning Sentinel* on the way to earning a graduate degree at the University of Maine. He was a guidance counselor at Waterville Junior High. He also ran a small construction company. Mathieu owned a collection of eighteenth-century tools and had used these to build a cabin in the Maine woods.[220] His local connection to the fort, his familiarity and interest, his expertise with eighteenth-century construction techniques and his large collection of period tools made him the logical choice for the project.

Mathieu, serving as chief contractor, assembled a team of twelve to rebuild the blockhouse to specifications. He hired Lew Pelletier of Winslow to be architect and engineer. He enlisted his brother Bob and his nephew Peter, both from Pennsylvania. He brought in William Lynch, a blacksmith specializing in eighteenth-century techniques. Further, he recruited experts in colonial architecture, Eric Ekholm and Robert Leone. Six others offered carpentry and general building skills.[221]

Before Mathieu began the project, Art Speiss and Lee Cranmer of the Maine Historic Preservation Commission conducted another archaeological dig. From late April to late May 1989, they dug four feet through the deposited river sediment. They uncovered more prehistoric artifacts, broken stones and several Native American hearths.[222] The archaeologists broke new ground and uncovered artifacts and remnants of great interest. Speiss described the site as "one of the state's richest historic troves" and added that the excavation felt like "peeling an onion," as each layer of buried earth revealed some rich window into the past inhabitants of Fort Point.[223]

Finally, with the latest archaeological digs complete, Mathieu began the restoration in early July. Using the architectural plans from the 1936 Historic American Buildings Survey and the original fort plans, Lew Pelletier drew up the blueprints for the restored blockhouse. Of the thirty-three original timbers that the state had recovered, only twenty-two were in good enough condition to be used in the restoration. Mathieu secured additional pine timbers from Scott Paper. To prevent against another disaster like the flood of 1987, Morrison Geotechnical Engineering drove small-diameter pipe piles twenty feet to the bedrock and then filled them with concrete.[224] With a steel plate welded on top to support the bottom logs, another steel rod was fastened upward, extending through all the timbers of the first story. Through this method, the restoration team ensured the safety and longevity of this precariously placed blockhouse.

"The repeated pop of wood being hewed with an ax, the faint sound of shingles being split with a hatchet, the hum of whittlers squaring logs, for further authenticity, add the droning clang of blacksmiths forging tools and hardware, followed with the steamy hiss of red-hot metal dipped into a

The rebuild begins, July 1988. *Stan Mathieu.*

Stan Mathieu during the blockhouse rebuild. *Stan Mathieu.*

wooden bucket full of cold water."[225] This is how Tony Cristan of the *Central Maine Morning Sentinel* described the unusual restoration. Dressed in period clothing, Mathieu's twelve-person team began the rebuild. Using tools like a foot adze, chalk lines, hand drill and broadaxe, they hewed the timbers into the right shape.[226]

Using an authentic colonial technique called tapered dovetails, Mathieu and his team carved notches in the end of each log to form a tightly interlocking system. Massey Lumber donated most of the other lumber required. While pine made up the walls, Mathieu used spruce for the truss system that held the roof and cedar for the shingles. Mortar and pegs helped to hold the doorframe securely in the wall. For the sake of authenticity, Mathieu included all the original cannon ports and horizontal slots for guns to rest while shooting. One gun port faced the Kennebec River on the north wall, while one faced southward on the Sebasticook River. The team included a door on the upper level, which to the modern observer seems to open to nothing. That door connected to the ramparts on a tall palisade wall. Inside the blockhouse, the builders rebuilt the staircase added in the nineteenth century and later repaired, making the upper floor accessible to visitors. Mathieu sacrificed modern conveniences in construction. He used metal nails only on the door—made by a blacksmith using period tools and techniques.[227]

On August 1, Mathieu and his team, in collaboration with the Friends of Fort Halifax, hosted a large community outreach at Fort Halifax Park. The Friends of Fort Halifax recruited members and raised funds for restoration efforts and events. At the suggestion of member H.A. "Rudy" Fougere, the Friends charged dues of $17.54, a fee related to the year of Fort Halifax's founding, for two years.[228] Leaders of the DAR, Winslow Historical Society, Knights of Columbus, VFW, Lions Club, Pattee Pond Association and others offered financial assistance. Mathieu and the team demonstrated various colonial building techniques for onlookers and for Maine media. Blacksmithing, fire building, colonial baking and tomahawk-throwing demonstrations brought eighteenth-century living to life.[229] A fourth archaeological dig began in late September, furthering interest in the site.[230]

As the restoration progressed through August, September and October, the blockhouse transformed significantly, resembling the commanding outpost that had existed during the French and Indian War. Several difficult aspects of the building remained—namely the truss system and the roof. Mathieu's carpenters, Erick Ekholm and Robert Leone, built the complex support system. A series of eight timbers came together supporting the kingpost and the roof. The kingpost, a five-foot-long beam that extends vertically from the topmost point of the blockhouse, had not existed since the 1850s. However, Mathieu

The roof system. *Stan Mathieu.*

Stan Mathieu outside the nearly rebuilt blockhouse, September 1989. *Stan Mathieu.*

included it in order to restore the fort to its earliest and most authentic form. Once the truss system was complete, the team fixed tightly tapered cedar shingles to the roof. The blockhouse was finished in late October.[231]

With the spirit of Winslow reinvigorated through this dramatic community effort, a grand rededication followed on October 30, 1988. Despite bitter cold, the day kicked off with a reenactment attended by over three hundred spectators.[232] Herb Hartman, the director of the Maine Bureau of Parks and Recreation, welcomed the crowd.[233] Don Carter of the Friends of Fort Halifax read a proclamation sent by the governor of Maine. Ed Meadows, the commissioner for the Maine Department of Conservation, read a proclamation sent by Massachusetts governor Michael Dukakis, then on the campaign trail. Each governor applauded the rebuilding efforts and reflected on New England's rich history. Perleston "Bud" Pert of the Maine Department of Education gave an overview of Fort Halifax. U.S. senator George Mitchell of Waterville spoke next. Mitchell reflected on the fort's significance and shared some childhood memories. Mitchell said, "The ground on which we stand was one of the most important sites in the state of Maine. It is important that we understand our heritage because we derive so much from it." His comments echoed the speech given by Governor Baxter at the DAR's

Senator George Mitchell speaks at the rededication ceremony, October 1988. *Stan Mathieu.*

1924 ceremony. As a youth, Mitchell remembered crossing the Two Cent Bridge. He "would come down to Fort Halifax and recreate the battles between soldiers and Indians."[234] Mitchell's sentiments showed that, for many, the ceremony and the entire restoration had invoked nostalgia, if not imagination, for Maine's heritage to a degree that had been felt few times before.

With the restoration complete and the rededication over, one final obstacle remained for the blockhouse: the National Historic Landmark designation. Before the Flood of 1987, only half of the original construction remained. However, considering the blockhouse had been almost totally lost or destroyed, the Park Service proposed stripping Fort Halifax of its designation.[235] De-designation would mean fewer funding opportunities and fewer visitors. It would likely dash the dreams of the Friends of Fort Halifax

Ed Bearss and Herb Hartman inspect the blockhouse, by Dick Maxwell, August, 1989. *Morning Sentinel.*

for something grander on the site. In short, de-designation threatened to demoralize the town and undermine Mathieu's achievement.

Consequently, the Friends of Fort Halifax, now with over one hundred committed members, began a vigorous campaign to maintain the blockhouse's designation. They joined with Earle G. Shettleworth Jr., director of the Maine Historic Preservation Commission, and drafted a preliminary master plan. Since Stan Mathieu had restored the fort as closely to the eighteenth-century original as possible, they argued, the historic landmark deserved to retain its designation. The Friends cited the 30 percent original timbers, the colonial building techniques, the kingpost and the roof construction as evidence that justified its continued recognition as a National Historic Landmark.[236]

The National Park Service sent chief historian Ed Bearss to visit the blockhouse and to write a report that would most likely determine its future. On August 23, state and local officials met with Bearss in a Waterville hotel. Later that afternoon, they traveled to Winslow and inspected the blockhouse. Bearss, who announced that he was a "direct descendent" of Major General John Winslow, was impressed by the "meticulous and thorough attention to using mid-eighteenth-century materials, design, and features." He commended the town's determination and persistence throughout restoration and the delisting scare. Bearss promptly issued a

Fort Halifax blockhouse, January 1989. *Stan Mathieu.*

report that ensured that the blockhouse maintained its place on the list of National Historic Landmarks.[237]

The period between April 1, 1987, and October 30, 1989, proved to be both uncertain and also momentous for the blockhouse's history. The April Fools' Day Flood had brought the fort to the verge of nonexistence. Instead, Fort Halifax lived on in an amazing effort to rebuild its blockhouse and to save it from de-designation. More importantly, the beautifully restored blockhouse represented far more than simply the physical materials and structure but the labor and dedication of Winslow's citizens. In a letter to Bearss, Representative Carter discussed the hidden value of these turbulent and transformative years: "I might also add that the Flood of '87 may yet prove to have been a 'blessing in disguise.' I say this because the loss of the Blockhouse and its subsequent restoration has created a tremendous amount of enthusiasm among the citizens of this State and Country."[238]

Chapter 9

Winslow's True Treasure: Fort Halifax Park since 1990

On Wednesday, July 25, 1990, six members of the Friends of Fort Halifax dressed in replica clothing they rented from an Augusta costume shop. To re-create the arrival of Major General Winslow's forces at Fort Point in 1754, they launched their canoes off Lithgow Street, a few hundred yards below the confluence of the Kennebec and Sebasticook. Laughing as they struggled against the strong current, they veered into the mouth of the Sebasticook and then headed toward the peninsula on which the Fort Halifax blockhouse and park now stood. Soon, they landed on Fort Point and marched to the blockhouse. Town librarian Priscilla Lee treated spectators to a mock interview with John Barber the militia clerk in 1754 (portrayed by Gerry Poissonier). In the following days, the Friends led reenactments of key moments in 1754. During the weekend, as in 1981, the fort hosted carnival booths, a petting zoo, archaeological and historical displays and live entertainment.[239]

Fort Halifax Days reflected the increased historical interest that the reconstruction project had generated. Amidst the de-designation talk, the 1989 preliminary master plan sparked a debate in its effort to sustain the momentum created by the rebuild. Like its 1974 predecessor, the 1989 master plan wanted to repackage Fort Halifax Park to emphasize its historical significance. However, the 1989 plan outdid its predecessor. It called for "full-scale reconstruction in-situ of all missing elements of the fort complex" and for on-site and off-site museums. Hoping to seize on the momentum of the rebuild, the master plan struck an optimistic tone: "It is exciting to think that

Friends of Fort Halifax at Fort Halifax Days, by Ron Maxwell, July 1990. *Morning Sentinel.*

the program initiated in 1987 is a continuation of more than a century of concern for this important site, and that the future will see the best possible research and interpretation on New England's remotest colonial fort."[240] What would it take for these goals to be realized?

Fort Halifax Days inspired, in 1991, the first Winslow Family Fourth of July Celebration at Fort Halifax Park. The town and the Friends welcomed home Gulf War veterans, opened up the blockhouse and displayed a cannon thought to be from the fort. The annual celebration has become the biggest event each year in central Maine.[241] Colby students once again took an interest in the blockhouse. Some visited on the weekends to relax and take in the scenery.[242] Archaeological explorations continued, too. In the fall of 1990, Lee Cranmer looked for the Fort House's cellars, chimney bases and floor supports. He found beautiful ceramics. He also concluded that Lithgow's fort was actually 115.5 feet square. Work in 1991 excavated the fort's food storage pit. In August 1994, the seventh dig since 1987 took place, yielding more ancient artifacts. In 1995, archaeologists found further evidence of the seventeenth-century trading post located just north of the fort and excavated Fort Halifax's privy. The Maine Historic Preservation Commission planned to return soon but never did.[243]

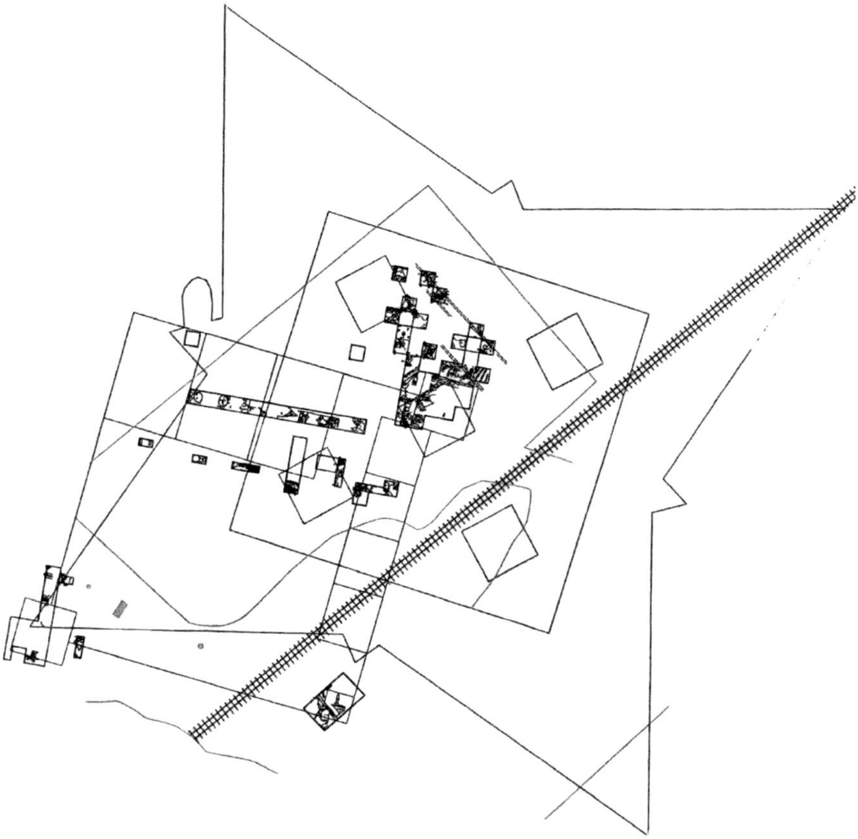

Fort Halifax digs, 1987–95. *Terrence J. DeWan & Associates.*

Despite these developments from 1990 to 1995, interest in expanding historical and recreational offerings at the fort slowly faded. No one explanation fits. Donald V. Carter, the driving force behind the Friends of Fort Halifax and its leading advocate with the State of Maine, died in a tragic car accident in December 1990. Winslow transitioned economically and demographically in the 1990s. Manufacturing jobs diminished, and the big plants closed, culminating in the merger of Scott Paper with Kimberly-Clark in 1995 and the closure of the paper mill in 1998. Many residents were distracted. Others were content with Fort Halifax Park as it was. After all, completing the park and restoring it after the flood had taken considerable effort and expense. For several years, save for the spectacular Fourth of July festivities, Fort Halifax Park was left largely to its own devices.[244]

Sign marking the entrance to Fort Halifax Park. *David Thomas.*

In 2002, a familiar notion reemerged: that of further developing Fort Halifax Park. As Winslow transitioned from a manufacturing center to a suburban community, some maintained that developing Fort Halifax Park might boost the town's economy. In 1974, Steve Clark and the Winslow Conservation Commission had called for a boat launch, walking trails, landscaping enhancement and more recreational opportunities.[245] In 1979, the VFW and the first Friends of Fort Halifax proposed that the new park "include a dock for boats and seaplane passenger facilities." The following year, the Maine National Guard offered to build an arched bridge to an island in the Kennebec River—the island where Lithgow's officers and their wives picnicked. And in June 1985, several men approached Parks and Recreation director Lee Breton and floated the possibility of starting a pleasure boat operation from Fort Halifax to Augusta. Fort Halifax Days and the Winslow Family Fourth of July Celebration had shown the site's popularity for community celebrations. The site's recreational value also increased. Visitors carved out small footpaths along the rivers as they snapped photos of the beautiful scenery and wildlife. The cleaner the Kennebec got, the more fishermen and kayakers enjoyed its waters.[246]

In 2002, the Maine Department of Transportation hired landscape engineers Terrence J. DeWan & Associates to create a future vision for Fort Halifax Park as part of its Kennebec-Chaudière International Corridor planning. This report was substantially more elaborate than past reports. Although the DeWan plan valued the history of Fort Halifax, it also sought to create "a neighborhood commercial setting." Landscape architects envisioned "an information kiosk at the entrance to the park," an "outline of Fort Halifax" and a "re-creation of a second blockhouse."[247] Could one deliberately make Fort Halifax Park into a moneymaking tourist destination while still maintaining its historical integrity?

DeWan & Associates' vision rejuvenated interest in Fort Halifax and its rebuilt blockhouse. In June 2004, Old Fort Western historic site organized a weekend-long reenactment. Some participants rowed the Fort Western bateau to Fort Halifax and back. About 120 people camped in Fort Halifax Park. Penobscot Indians returned to Fort Halifax to partake in the events.

Blockhouse with the new bandstand in the background. *David Thomas.*

But excitement for the park and its many uses was not without controversy.[248] In the spring of 2005, the Fourth of July Committee hastily constructed a bandstand at Fort Halifax Park over the objections of the Maine Historic Preservation Commission.[249]

The bandstand project was debated in newspapers and in public. It rallied the Friends of Fort Halifax, now led by Gerry Poissonier, to vigorously promote the historical importance of the site. The Friends helped the town to secure a grant from the Maine Department of Transportation for a new sign at the entrance to Fort Halifax Park.[250] In 2006, it reprinted and distributed more than two hundred copies of Carleton Fisher's 1972 booklet on Fort Halifax. In May of that year, it met with town officials to pitch a new plan for partially rebuilding the fort and moving the existing parking lot that overlapped the imprint of Lithgow's fort. The Friends also hired DeWan & Associates to devise a more detailed plan for the future of Fort Halifax Park.[251]

At the same time, the town began to reevaluate its long-term plans. In 2007, it organized a Comprehensive Planning Committee. Committee members polled residents that summer. By October of that year, the Friends and DeWan & Associates had unveiled a new vision for the park. They proposed to add interpretive signage, relocate the existing parking lots, mark the outline of the fort with granite blocks and rebuild some of the palisade. Part-time volunteers would staff the park during the summer. They would add a museum on-site and build a trail along the river north to the Two Cent Bridge and south toward Augusta.[252] When the Planning Committee issued its official report in 2008, it, too, concluded that Fort Halifax was an asset to the community largely because of its historical roots, not because it was frequently used as a recreational area. "Fort Halifax is the symbol of the town, and should therefore be singled out for individual attention and resources in preservation and education," the committee said. The Friends of Fort Halifax and the Winslow Comprehensive Planning Committee envisioned Fort Halifax Park as a site for historical and educational opportunities, and they expected the town to appropriate money for that purpose.[253]

A lack of widespread consensus, a national recession and the difficulty of arranging with Pan Am Railways to move the railway crossing stalled this plan. Before long, the Winslow Family Fourth of July Committee devised a counter report of its own in 2009, a report that reflected some rather different interests. The committee members did not ignore educational opportunities and historical appreciation. But they wanted to use Fort Halifax Park to boost the local economy: "Since the development of Bangor's Waterfront

Park it is apparent that projects of this nature boost the economy and it is our intent to do the same with Winslow's historical Halifax waterfront."[254] They proposed building Fort Halifax look-alike "picnic table Gazebos along the new walking path." Barbecue pits could be added. They revived the concept of a "River Boat [that would] benefit the community by attracting tourist[s] to the area."[255] Who would pay for these developments? Could taxpayers bear the burden? Could the Friends and the Fourth of July Committee see eye to eye?

During early 2010, the Fourth of July Committee and the Friends, each with noble but divergent goals, pursued different agendas. The Fourth of July Committee, in Chairman Ron LeClair's last year at the helm, tried to build a two-story sound stage. The Friends shot down that idea. In the spring, committee members and volunteers cleared an additional four acres along the Kennebec "covered in dense brush and dead tree limbs, and littered with old tires, glass and trash." They improved the beauty of the park. Later that summer, they offered movie nights in the park. Critics grumbled that the group had lacked the proper permits and permissions. As one member of the Friends of Fort Halifax claimed, "the Fourth of July group is running too hard and too fast." Some residents also thought the celebration was getting too big.[256]

At the same time, the Friends of Fort Halifax considered funding more costly archaeological work in the area where the barracks once stood and then decided against it. In light of the Fourth of July Committee's recent activities, the Friends again hired DeWan for more in-depth planning in 2010. If visitors arrived, they insisted, it should be to appreciate the history and beauty of Fort Halifax and its vicinity. The Friends' goals included to: "protect and preserve the park's rich archaeological resources"; to "display the original footprint of Fort Halifax"; to "treat the park as an outdoor classroom for learning as well as recreation"; to "improve the appearance of the park from Route 201"; and to "promote an uncluttered, quiet, and natural environment within the park." The educational aspect was crucial because "there is precious little education on-site, and most people visiting would be unable to understand that the fort was actually much larger than the blockhouse." Fort Halifax would attract more visitors yet maintain its historical image and reputation. The Friends also sought to raise awareness of Native American life at Fort Point. They consulted with Indian leaders on how best to do that. An Indian longhouse and canoes would be among several "interactive displays to serve as focal points in strategic areas of the park." Artifacts, tools and exhibits would be on display. The blockhouse would be open for tours. This 2010 report, more so than any of its predecessors, offered a plan geared at making Fort Halifax Park an "outdoor classroom."[257]

Now, Fort Halifax was so important that the townspeople were fighting over it. Each year, the Fourth of July Committee had created a family-friendly environment that brought the community together unlike ever before. And the Friends had a plan that would benefit Winslow businesses and students alike.

Community members were concerned that a boat launch would be too dangerous; the water was too shallow and the currents too swift. Many people remembered a near drowning at the point in 2004, when Doug Handy—a legally blind fisherman angling for stripers—rescued a nine-year-old boy being swept away by the current.[258]

Another anonymous citizen, apparently unaware of the reinforced steel anchoring the rebuilt blockhouse, criticized both the Friends of Fort Halifax and the Fourth of July Committee and asked the *Morning Sentinel*, "If the plan to build replicas of the original Fort Halifax complex goes through, what happens when the next flood washes them away as well?" In the same letter, the anonymous author wrote, "Ask not what your remnants can do for you but what you can do for your remnants." The resident worried that any grand improvements would be destroyed eventually by floods and in the meantime would ruin the "tranquil nature of the park." Other Winslow residents worried about erosion on the Sebasticook and thought that preserving and repairing the blockhouse should be a more immediate concern.[259]

In June 2010, the town council created a committee to reconcile residents' contrasting visions and to build a consensus plan for the future of the Fort Halifax blockhouse and park. Committee members included town officials, representatives from the Fourth of July Committee and the Friends of Fort Halifax, teachers and students. As the committee worked, Maine Parks installed a new interpretive display by the blockhouse and agreed to open the fort to the public in 2011. The committee's work culminated in a seventh plan, written and illustrated by Terrence J. DeWan & Associates in June 2011.[260]

The 2011 DeWan plan compared six of the previous plans. Each one "stated the importance of promoting the history of Fort Halifax at the park." It made clear its vision: to "preserve and promote all of the unique historical aspects of the park" and to "display the location of Fort Halifax's original footprint." The park would become an "outdoor classroom" for Winslow and Colby students. It aimed to "improve recreational opportunities in the

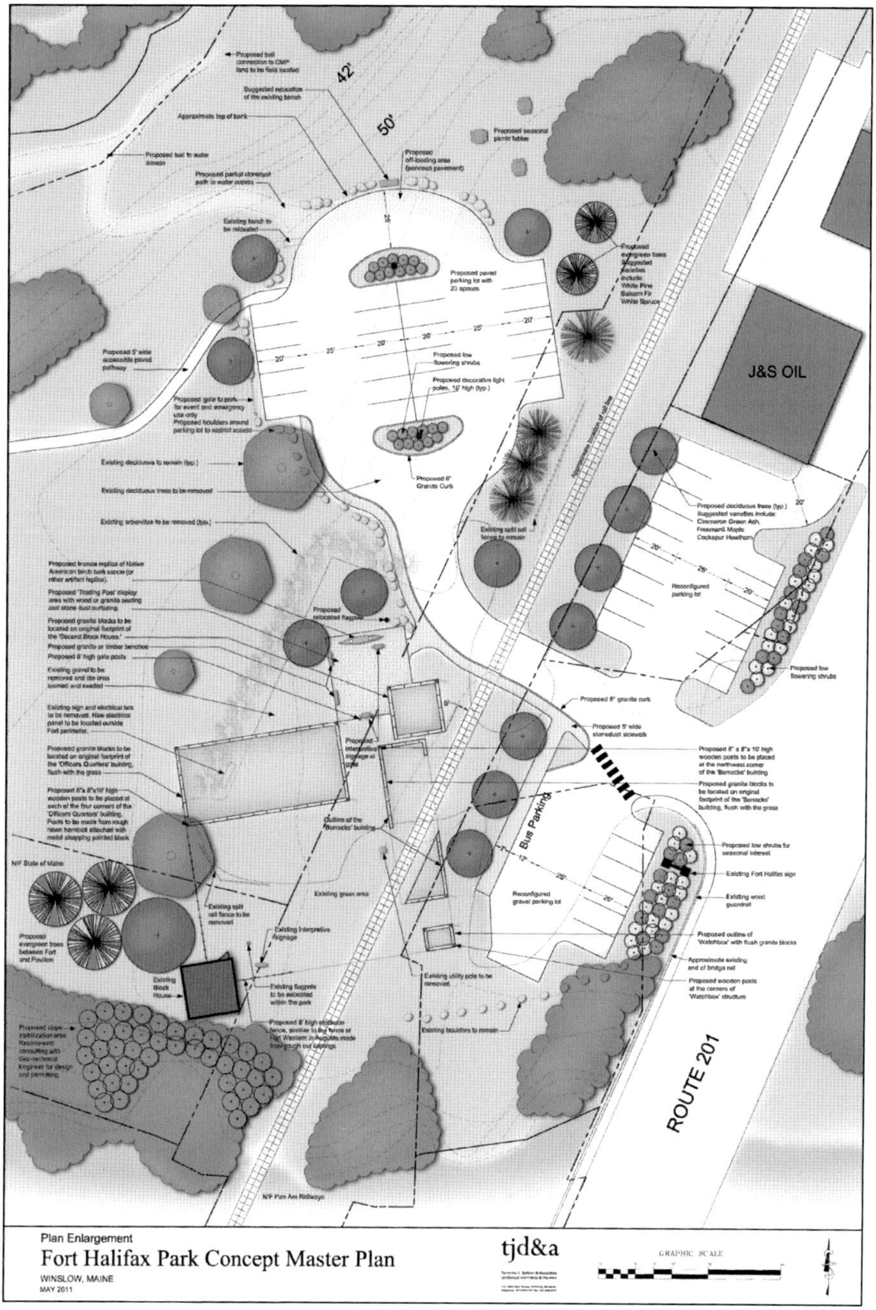

Blowup view of the Fort Halifax Park concept master plan, 2011. *Terrence J. DeWan & Associates.*

Aerial view of the Fort Halifax Park concept master plan, 2011. *Terrence J. DeWan & Associates.*

park." Yet it would "maintain the open spaces within the park." As Ray Caron, Winslow town councilor and committee chair stated, "This plan capitalizes on the uniqueness of this site for the benefit of all."[261]

The town council authorized a Fort Halifax Park Implementation Committee, and it met on multiple occasions from 2011 to 2013. Despite the best efforts of town manager Mike Heavener, grant money proved elusive as a national and state economic recession continued. That all seemed to change in 2014, however, when the Maine Bureau of Parks and Lands approved a massive grant proposal geared to implement much of the 2011 master plan.[262] In early 2014, however, much work remained to upgrade Fort Halifax Park, and its future remained full of possibilities.

Conclusion

On Thanksgiving morning in 2008, Gerald Cates drove to Fort Halifax Park to inspect the water level after some flooding. Though he called himself a "sportsman and conservationist," Cates had no idea how to handle the situation he encountered. A man was standing on the shore with an injured seal at his feet. Cates called the Winslow Police. Officer Josh Veilleux thought someone was either imagining things or playing a practical joke. But when he arrived on the scene, he discovered that not only was the caller correct, but also a small crowd had formed. Officer Veilleux contacted the Maine Warden Service, which arrived an hour later—just after the seal returned to the river. It would seem that that was the end of the matter.[263]

The seal reappeared the next day less than a mile upstream, on the west bank of the Kennebec River, near the Hathaway Building in Waterville. According to a biologist for the Maine Department of Marine Resources, "The seal's mouth was torn and bleeding…its left eye appeared inflamed or infected." Furthermore, the seal was malnourished. The dazed, injured and starving seal was brought to a rehabilitation center in Biddeford.[264] Amazingly, in less than a month, the seal, which had been affectionately nicknamed Nero, was well on his way to recovery.[265] Since Fort Halifax's encounter with Nero, other seals have appeared near Fort Halifax Park, swimming along the Kennebec and the Sebasticook Rivers and even coming ashore.

Incidents such as Nero's encounter with Fort Point have called attention to the fact that Fort Halifax Park is bustling with wildlife. In addition to lost

Crowds gather for music and fireworks at Fort Halifax Park, 2013. *Winslow Family Fourth of July Celebration.*

harbor seals, the old blockhouse hosts black tern, bald eagle, woodchuck and rare orchids. Fishermen gather in the evenings at the confluence of the Kennebec and Sebasticook. As one reporter put it, at least "11 fish species including striped bass, American sturgeon, shortnose sturgeon, American shad, rainbow [smelt], Atlantic salmon, alewife, blueback herring, American eel, tommycod, and sea lamprey" all "have free passage way to Waterville's Ticonic Bay." Conditions improved for alewives with the removal of the Fort Halifax Dam on the Sebasticook in 2008. These rivers invite kayak and canoe competitions, all within sight of the old blockhouse.[266]

In the twenty-first century, offerings at Fort Halifax Park have expanded. Unlike ever before, more visitors of all ages and backgrounds now enjoy the land and the fort's remnant, and this is largely the result of the continued work by the Fourth of July Committee and Winslow Public Works. The town's Fourth of July Celebration has become the largest in the state.[267]

The blockhouse clearly holds a special place in the hearts of many of Winslow's residents. On any given day, visitors to Fort Halifax Park might see avid fishermen, young couples on a picnic, a grandparent relating the

Fort Halifax blockhouse, 2012. *Author photo.*

history of Fort Halifax or their own memories of the remaining blockhouse to an interested grandchild. Some have even shared their most cherished moments at Fort Halifax. In 2010, reported Dennis Dacus, Winslow Parks and Recreation director, Fort Halifax Park was "home to over 25 weddings… Multiple business picnics, church gatherings, fundraising endeavors, and birthday parties." In the 2010s, YouTube videos, Twitter updates and digital photos were daily made at Fort Halifax.[268]

Much lies ahead for the remnant of Fort Halifax and the park that bears its name. Fort Halifax embodies the spirit of the town of Winslow. It has served many roles over the years, decades and now centuries. But it has always defined the identity of the town that loves and cherishes it. With the help of local caregivers through many generations, the final standing blockhouse of Fort Halifax has withstood floods, mistreatment and neglect. It has stood the test of time. It is a testament to the will and spirit of the town that has fought to preserve it for future generations to enjoy, study and marvel upon that "venerable relic" that continues to reinvent itself but remains the enduring symbol of the town of Winslow.[269]

Appendix A Timeline of Events

3000 BCE–1692 CE	Indians inhabit the area that later becomes the site of Fort Halifax.
1620	The Pilgrims arrive, and Plymouth Colony is founded.
1625	Edward Winslow trades with Indians along the Kennebec River.
1629	The Plymouth Council grants the Kennebec Patent to the Pilgrim Colony.
1653–54	Traders build posts on Fort Point and opposite it on the south bank of the Sebasticook.
1661	The Kennebec Patent is sold to the Kennebec Proprietors.
1676	Tensions flare between Indians and colonists in New England; Kennebec Indians murder trader Richard Hammond and take dozens of white settlers as prisoners.
1678	A treaty is signed at Casco Bay, ending King Philip's War. White prisoners are released.
1692	Major Benjamin Church burns the Indian village at Taconnet to the ground.

1749	Dr. Silvester Gardiner and other Boston merchants purchase the Kennebec Patent from the heirs of the Plymouth Company.
1754–63	The French and Indian War/Seven Years' War takes place.
1754	Major General John Winslow constructs Fort Halifax.
1755–56	Captain William Lithgow modifies and completes Fort Halifax.
1755–57	Indian attacks on the Kennebec unsettle Fort Halifax.
1761	British military engineer John Montresor visits Fort Halifax on a surveying expedition.
1764	A surveying expedition under Joseph Chadwick visits Fort Halifax.
1767	Massachusetts disbands the garrison at Fort Halifax.
1770	Dr. Gardiner purchases the fort and surrounding lands.
1771	Winslow officially becomes a town, and its town meeting takes place at Fort Halifax.
1775	Dr. Gardiner leases Fort Halifax and the adjoining land to Ephraim Ballard.
1775	Benedict Arnold stops at Fort Halifax with over 1,100 men on their way to Quebec.
1776	The Winslow Committee of Safety expels Ephraim Ballard and seizes Fort Halifax.
1779–83	The ruins of the fort host militiamen, a trader and Penobscot Indians.
1798	Richard Thomas tears down the Fort House and builds an inn, the Halifax House. Settlers disassemble most of the fort, except for the blockhouse on the Sebasticook.
1798	Dr. Gardiner's heir, Robert Hallowell, recovers Fort Halifax and the surrounding land. The property changes hands several times over the next several decades.
1802	Waterville separates from Winslow.

1813	Waterville College is founded. It later becomes Colby University and then Colby College.
1814	The "Clinton Raid" takes place; settlers assemble at Fort Halifax.
1845	Asa Redington Jr. delivers the fort's cornerstone to the Maine Statehouse.
1852	Timothy Paine conducts archaeological research at Fort Halifax and publishes a series of newspaper articles on his discoveries.
1855	Hiram Simpson buys several lots, including the blockhouse. The following year, he deeds the blockhouse to Asa Redington Jr.
1867	The *Waterville Mail* decries the condition of the blockhouse. Redington Jr. sells the blockhouse to the Ticonic Water and Power Company.
1873–74	Three local men repair the remaining blockhouse.
1875	The Lockwood Company buys the land from the Ticonic Water and Power Company.
1876	Historian William Goold visits Fort Halifax.
1890	Edward Ware builds a sawmill at Fort Point.
1891	Hollingsworth & Whitney mill is built.
1893	A *Colby Echo* article laments the poor condition of the blockhouse.
1901	A devastating flood destroys the Two Cent Bridge, but the blockhouse survives.
1902	Maine Central Railroad buys land from the Lockwood Company and builds a railroad bridge over the Sebasticook.
1905	The old blockhouse survives a fire caused by a freight train wreck.
1913	The Fort Halifax chapter, DAR, is formed; it raises the American flag over Fort Halifax.

1916	The Good Will-Hinckley boys visit Fort Halifax.
1919	Evidence of the Red Paint Indians is found at Fred Lancaster's nearby farm.
1921	Winslow holds its sesquicentennial at the blockhouse.
1924	In a ceremony attended by Governor Percival Baxter and by a descendant of Dr. Gardiner, the Maine Central Railroad relinquishes ownership of the blockhouse to the DAR.
1936	A flood damages the blockhouse walls. The Historic American Buildings Survey produces detailed architectural sketches of the blockhouse.
1948	The DAR receives an award for its service that it puts toward a new sign.
1954	The DAR marks the 200th anniversary of Fort Halifax with a politicized ceremony on site.
1956	Central Maine Railroad donates a new flagpole.
1960	The nearby Fort Halifax Bridge is completed over the Sebasticook.
1962	A state representative inspects the blockhouse and calls it a "priceless gem."
1966	The DAR officially transfers ownership of Fort Halifax to the State of Maine.
1968	Fort Halifax becomes a National Historic Landmark and joins the National Register of Historic Places.
1970	Interest builds in creating Fort Halifax Park.
1972	Carleton E. Fisher publishes *History of Fort Halifax*.
1974	The Winslow Conservation Commission provides the vision for Fort Halifax Park.
1975	The Arnold Bicentennial Expedition stops at Fort Halifax.
1977	The State of Maine repairs the blockhouse and re-shingles the roof.

1979	MacCrillis-Rousseau VFW Post leads efforts to create Fort Halifax Park.
1981	Fort Halifax Park is officially opened.
1983	Winslow acquires the warehouse on Fort Point from Pine Tree Furniture.
1987	The blockhouse is washed away by a massive flood. Lee Cranmer and archaeologists explore the site of Fort Halifax. They return seven more times through 1995.
1988	Stan Mathieu rebuilds the blockhouse. A rededication ceremony is held in late October.
1989	The reconstructed blockhouse defends and retains its designation as a National Historic Landmark.
1990	Fort Halifax Days is held at the fort.
1991	Fort Halifax Park hosts the first Winslow Family Fourth of July Celebration.
1997	H.A. "Rudy" Fougere paints Fort Halifax as it looked in the 1750s.
2002	DeWan & Associates presents a plan for updates to Fort Halifax Park for the Kennebec-Chaudière International Corridor project.
2004	A historic encampment is held at Fort Halifax Park. The Old Fort Western bateau travels from that fort to Fort Halifax and back.
2005	A new sign for Fort Halifax Park is installed.
2006–07	The Friends of Fort Halifax devises a new plan for Fort Halifax Park.
2008	The Fort Halifax Dam is removed on the Sebasticook. The Town of Winslow addresses the future of Fort Halifax in its comprehensive plan. Nero the harbor seal visits Fort Halifax.
2009	Winslow's Fourth of July Committee presents a plan concerning Fort Halifax Park.

2010	The Friends of Fort Halifax and DeWan & Associates devise a plan for Fort Halifax Park. Maine Parks installs an interpretive sign.
2010–11	The Fort Halifax Park Planning Committee, working with DeWan & Associates, builds a consensus on what should be done with Fort Halifax Park. An Implementation Committee is formed to seek funding for the plan.
2014	*Fort Halifax: Winslow's Historic Outpost* is published. Park upgrade implementation continues.

Appendix B

Fort Halifax Namesakes

The following organizations, businesses and landmarks, based in Winslow unless otherwise noted, named themselves after Fort Halifax and the men associated with the original fort. Some of these namesakes have come and gone. Others, like the old blockhouse, have stood the test of time.

Canton Halifax Masonic Lodge
Fort Halifax ATV Club
Fort Halifax Band
Fort Halifax Bridge
Fort Halifax Commons
Fort Halifax Construction (in Waterville)
Fort Halifax Dam
Fort Halifax Feeds (in Burnham)
Fort Halifax Gasoline & Fuel Oil Company
Fort Halifax Grange #583
Fort Halifax Grocery
Fort Halifax Hill Road
Fort Halifax Inn
Fort Halifax Lodge, No. 9, Independent Order of Odd Ladies
Fort Halifax Miniature Golf Course
Fort Halifax Motor Company
Fort Halifax Packing Company
Fort Halifax Poultry Company

Fort Halifax Packing Company, by Ron Maxwell, 1987. *Morning Sentinel.*

Fort Halifax Power Company
Fort Halifax Redemption & Beverage
Fort Halifax School, on Lithgow Street
Fort Halifax Snowdrifters
Fort Halifax Tavern
Halifax Crossing shopping plaza
Halifax House inn
Halifax Lodge, International Organization of Good Templars
Halifax (steamship)
Halifax Street/School
Pattee Pond/Road
Town of Winslow

Notes

Chapter 1

1. Florence S. Demers, "Indian Burial Ground Found on Sebasticook River Bank," Kim Leighton, "Prehistoric Ft. Halifax Served Indians as Local Fish Store," *Central Maine Morning Sentinel*, July 10, 1976, April 25, 1989; "The Sebasticook Watershed"; Calvert, *Dawn over the Kennebec*, 19.
2. Dwayne Rioux, "Silent Hunters Stalked the Kennebec," *Central Maine Morning Sentinel*, November 2, 1991.
3. Calvert, *Dawn over the Kennebec*, 14.
4. Dwayne Rioux, "Mountains, Lakes, & Rivers Echo Abenaki Names," *Central Maine Morning Sentinel*, November 9, 1991.
5. "Indian Fort at Taconic," 1, in VF #90450, Winslow Public Library; Goold, "Fort Halifax," 215, 235; Marriner, Little Talks #913, December 26, 1971, http://web.colby.edu/specialcollections/2011/02/02/lt913-readonly.
6. Hakluyt and Purchas, *Hakluytus Posthumus*, 19:404.
7. Caldwell, *Rivers of Fortune*, 63.
8. Whittemore, *Centennial History of Waterville*, 33.
9. Mitchell and Davis, *Winslow Register*, 6.
10. Kingsbury, "Town of Winslow," 537–38.
11. Marriner, Little Talks #913, December 26, 1971; Caldwell, *Rivers of Fortune*, 65; Davis and Mitchell, *Winslow Register*, 37.
12. Richard A. Pierce, "The Fort-Halifax Days before the Fort," *Central Maine Morning Sentinel*, October 12, 1987.
13. Caldwell, *Rivers of Fortune*, 67.
14. Whittemore, *Centennial History of Waterville*, 42; Pierce, "Fort-Halifax Days."

15. Whittemore, *Centennial History of Waterville*, 42–43.
16. Marriner, Little Talks #520, January 7, 1962, http://web.colby.edu/specialcollections/2010/12/21/lt520-readonly.
17. Mitchell and Davis, *Winslow Register*, 20; *Journals of the House of Representatives of Massachusetts*, 30:97, 121 (December 5, 14, 1753); Resolve, January 4, 1754, *MAR*, 15:96–97.

Chapter 2

18. Barber, "Journal," 281–82, 283n.
19. Goold, "Fort Halifax," 221; Marriner, Little Talks #520.
20. Shirley, Speech, March 28, 1754, *DHSM*, 12:246–52; Goold, "Fort Halifax," 215–17.
21. Shirley to Jonathan Bane, April 11, 15, 1754; Shirley to North, April 25, 1754, *DHSM*, 12:249–50, 261–62; Fisher, *Fort Halifax*, 4.
22. Shirley, Speech, March 28, October 18, 1754, *DHSM*, 12:246–52, 321–23; Fisher, *Fort Halifax*, 1–2.
23. Shirley, Speech, October 18, 1754, *DHSM*, 12:323.
24. Goold, "Fort Halifax," 221n–222n, 223.
25. Kershaw, *Kennebeck Proprietors*, 90; Fisher, *Fort Halifax*, 3–4, 21, 27n; *Pennsylvania Journal*, October 10, 1754; Dow, *Fort Western*, 26–30; the Committee of the Plymouth Company to Gershom Flagg, May 1754, and Articles of Agreement, May 7, 1754, Plymouth Company Records, Maine Historical Society, Coll. 60, Box 1, Folder 10.
26. Extracts from Message of June 4, 1754, *DHSM*, 12:281–82; Resolves, April 11, June 5, 1754, *MAR*, 15:144, 174; Goold, "Fort Halifax," 215, 218–19, 235.
27. Goold, "Fort Halifax," 223–24; Horne, *Winslow*, 28–30.
28. Shirley, Speech, October 18, 1754, *DHSM*, 12:327.
29. Goold, "Fort Halifax," 224–35, 233n-234n; Fisher, *Fort Halifax*, 5.
30. Barber, "Journal," 283–84; John Winslow, Deposition on the Kennebec River, May 3, 1755, http://www.mainememory.net/media/pdf/22545.pdf; Fisher, *Fort Halifax*, 27n.
31. Winslow, Deposition.
32. Barber, "Journal," 284; Articles of Agreement, July 6, 1754, Massachusetts Archives, 74:214; Fisher, *Fort Halifax*, 4–5, 10, 27n; Fuller, "Fort Halifax," 51–52; Marriner, Little Talks, #886, March 28, 1971, http://web.colby.edu/specialcollections/2011/01/25/lt886-readonly; Kershaw, *Kennebeck Proprietors*, 131; Horne, *Winslow*, 64–66.
33. *Journals of the House of Representatives of Massachusetts*, 32, pt. 1:29, 30 (June 5, 1755).

34. *Boston Gazette*, September 8, 1754; Shirley, Speech, October 18, 1754, *DHSM*, 12:324–25; Barber, "Journal," 285; Kershaw, *Kennebeck Proprietors*, 7, 131–32; Fisher, *Fort Halifax*, 4–5.
35. Fuller, "Fort Halifax," 51–52; Shirley to Willard, August 29, 1754, Massachusetts Archives, 54:315; Fisher, *Fort Halifax*, 5, 27n.
36. "Extract of a Letter from a Gentleman at Falmouth," *Boston Weekly News-Letter*, September 12, 1754, cited in Kershaw, *Kennebeck Proprietors*, 131; Goold, "Fort Halifax," 242, 242n; Fisher, *Fort Halifax*, 6.
37. Fisher, *Fort Halifax*, 8; Goold, "Fort Halifax," 281–82, 281n-282n; Paine, "Historical Sketch," November 25, 1852; Nason, *Old Colonial Houses*, 72.
38. "From Boston News Letter, 26th Sept., 1754," 174; Anderson, *Crucible of War*, 34–36, 38, 70; Speck, "Dunk, George Montagu, second earl of Halifax (1716–1771)."
39. "From Boston News Letter, 26th Sept., 1754," 174; Kershaw, *Kennebeck Proprietors*, 131, 138.
40. "BOSTON, September 16," *South Carolina Gazette*, October 17, 1754; Shirley, Speech, October 18, 1754, *DHSM*, 12:326; Goold, "Fort Halifax," 241–43; Fisher, *Fort Halifax*, 10.
41. Petition of Thomas Lawrence, October 30, 1754, Massachusetts Archives, 74:258–60; Resolve, November 2, 1755, *MAR*, 15:205; Goold, "Fort Halifax," 250n.
42. John Winslow, Plan of Fort Halifax, October 4, 1754, Massachusetts Archives, 74:471; Shirley, Speech, October 18, 1754, *DHSM*, 12:320–32; Fisher, *Fort Halifax*, 5–6, 10, 12–13; Goold, "Fort Halifax," 207n, 241.
43. Williams to Shirley, October 30, 1754, *Correspondence of William Shirley*, 2:102; Fisher, *Fort Halifax*, 16; Muster Roll, William Lithgow, 1754–56, 1756–57, Massachusetts Archives, 94:245, 95:208.
44. Shirley, Message to the House, November 6, 1754; Shirley, Warrant to Captain Lithgow, November 12, 1754, *DHSM*, 12:333–34, 12:336; Resolves, November 12, December 24, 26, 1754, *MAR*, 15:215, 244, 246–47; Coolidge and Smith, *Colonial Entrepreneur*, 117–18.
45. Whittemore, *Centennial History of Waterville*, 47; Shirley, Message to the House, November 11, 1754; Lithgow to Shirley, January 9, 1755, *DHSM*, 12:335–36, 341; Goold, "Fort Halifax," 244; Fisher, *Fort Halifax*, 18.

CHAPTER 3

46. Bernard, Message to the House, September 13, 1762, *DHSM*, 13:293; Hopkins, "The Lithgow Family," 15; Thayer, "The Lithgow Immigrants," 70–73; Fisher, *Fort Halifax*, 11, 20, 27n; Horne, *Winslow*, 66, 82–84, 86; Goold, "Fort Halifax," 206, 238, 284–85; Allen, *History of Dresden*, 168–69.

47. *Journals of the House of Representatives of Massachusetts*, 31:172–73 (December 23, 1754); Shirley to Lithgow, January 3, 1755, *DHSM*, 12:339–40; Goold, "Fort Halifax," 244n–246n, 246; William Lithgow, Petition, August 1756, Massachusetts Archives, 76:24; Resolve, November 6, 1759, *MAR*, 16:420; Fisher, *Fort Halifax*, 11, 22.
48. Winslow, Petition, December 4, 1754, cited in Goold, "Fort Halifax," 249n–250n; Lithgow to Wheelwright, June 14, 1755, *DHSM*, 12:417.
49. Lithgow to Shirley, January 9, 1755, *DHSM*, 12:340–43; "Personal Notes: Dr. John Calef"; Resolve, August 26, 1757, *MAR*, 16:57–58; Goold, "Fort Halifax," 246–47, 277; Fisher, *Fort Halifax*, 23–24.
50. Resolve, January 2, 1755, *MAR*, 15:251; Fisher, *Fort Halifax*, 20–22; Lithgow to Shirley, January 9, [March] 1755, *DHSM*, 12:340–43, 13:15-17; Goold, "Fort Halifax," 246–47; Hopkins, "The Lithgow Family," 8–10.
51. Shirley to Denny and Watts, January 18, 1755; Shirley to Lithgow, January 18, 1755, *DHSM*, 12:344, 344–45.
52. Lithgow to Shirley, January 9, February 20, 1755, *DHSM*, 12:342–43, 364.
53. Lithgow to Shirley, February 20, 1755, *DHSM*, 12:364–75; Coolidge and Smith, *Colonial Entrepreneur*, 119–20; Fisher, *Fort Halifax*, 11, 15–16; Goold, "Fort Halifax," 257–58.
54. Lithgow to Shirley, February 27, 1755, quoted in Fisher, *Fort Halifax*, 11; *Journals of the House of Representatives of Massachusetts*, 31, pt. 1:106 (June 21, 1755); Goold, "Fort Halifax," 259–60.
55. Lithgow to Shirley, February 20, 21, March 22, April 19, May 11, June 8, 1755; Lithgow to J. Wheelwright, June 14, 1755; Lithgow to Phips, July 18, 1755, *DHSM*, 12:364–75, 375, 380–83, 387–90, 391–93, 402–5, 417–18, 449–52; Fisher, *Fort Halifax*, 21–22.
56. Lithgow to Phips, July 18, 1755, *DHSM*, 12:451; Paine, "Historical Sketch," November 4, 11, 18, 25, 1852; Fisher, *Fort Halifax*, 14–15; Goold, "Fort Halifax," 280; Kingsbury, "Town of Winslow," 541. Archaeologists suspect that either Lithgow rotated Winslow's blockhouse forty-five degrees or Winslow had not built it exactly according to plan. Cranmer, "Blockhouses and Cellars," 23.
57. Shirley to Lithgow, July 15, 1755; Lithgow to J. Wheelwright, July 18, 1755; Lithgow to Phips, July 18, 1755; Phips, Message to the Council and House of Representatives, *DHSM*, 12:444–45, 447–49, 450–52, 459–61, 13:3–4.
58. Resolve, August 14, 1755, *MAR*, 15:377; Goold, "Fort Halifax," 266.
59. Lithgow to Willard, October 17, 1755; Goodwin to Phips, October 17, 1755; Lithgow to Phips, October 18, 1755, *DHSM*, 13:7, 7–9, 10–11; Paine, "Historical Sketch," November 4, 18, 1852; Goold, "Fort Halifax," 274; Fisher, *Fort Halifax*, 15.
60. Resolves, December 20, 1754, April 9, 1755, *MAR*, 15:241, 495–96; Goold, "Fort Halifax," 244–45, 275, 276n; Fisher, *Fort Halifax*, 6, 15; Paine, "Historical Sketch," November 4, 1852.

61. Paine, "Historical Sketch," November 4, 1852.
62. Lithgow to Willard, October 17, 1755, *DHSM*, 13:7.
63. Lithgow to Phips, October 20, 1755, *DHSM*, 13:11–12; Muster Roll, William Lithgow, 1754–56, Massachusetts Archives, 94:245.
64. Shirley to Lithgow, January 3, 1755, *DHSM*, 12:340; Resolve, February 11, 1766, *MAR*, 18:92; Fisher, *Fort Halifax*, 18.
65. "BOSTON, August 19," *Pennsylvania Gazette*, August 29, 1765.
66. "BOSTON, November 11," *Pennsylvania Gazette*, November 21, 1754; "Boston, dated March 29, 1755," *Boston Gazette*, May 29, 1755; Muster Roll, James Howard, 1755–56, Massachusetts Archives, 94:245; Lithgow to Goodwin, May 11, May 13, September 9, 1755, *DHSM*, 12:391–92, 393–95, 463–64; Resolves, June 10, November 1, 1755, *MAR*, 15:343, 396; Goold, "Fort Halifax," 243, 271; Fisher, *Fort Halifax*, 18, 21.
67. Shirley, Message to the House, December 10, 1754, *DHSM*, 12:338; Shirley to Lawrence, January 6, 1755, quoted in Goold, "Fort Halifax," 244; Hamilton to Gardiner, December 2, 1755, Massachusetts Archives, 55:108; Fisher, *Fort Halifax*, 16, 18; Mitchell and Davis, *Winslow Register*, 22.
68. Fisher, *Fort Halifax*, 16.
69. De Watteville, *British Soldier*.
70. Resolves, March 27, 1760, January 27, 1761, *MAR*, 16:512–13, 674; De Watteville, *British Soldier*.
71. Lithgow to Shirley, June 8, 1755, *DHSM*, 12:404–5; Hopkins, "The Lithgow Family," 1; Thayer, "The Lithgow Immigrants," 80; Allen, *History of Dresden*, 174.
72. Muster Roll, William Lithgow, 1752–54, 1754–56, 1756–57, 1757–58, Massachusetts Archives, 93:128, 94:245, 95:408–10, 96:189–90, Muster Roll, James Howard, 1756–57, Ibid., 95:411.
73. Lithgow, Petition, August 1756, Massachusetts Archives, 76:24; Resolve, November 6, 1759, *MAR*, 16:420; Fisher, *Fort Halifax*, 22; Muster Roll, William Lithgow, 1760–61, Massachusetts Archives, 99:2.
74. Shirley Message to the House, August 26, 27, 1756, *DHSM*, 13:38–39; Goold, "Fort Halifax," 266, 270–71.
75. James Howard to Shirley, June 12, 1756, *DHSM*, 13:32–33; Fisher, *Fort Halifax*, 19, 28n; Muster Roll, William Lithgow, 1756–57, Massachusetts Archives, 95:408.
76. Lithgow to Phips, May 23, 1757, in Goold, "Fort Halifax," 270.
77. "BOSTON, May 30," *Pennsylvania Gazette*, June 9, 1757; Lithgow to the Council, May 23, 1757, *DHSM*, 13:69–70.
78. James Howard to the Council, May 18, 1757; Goodwin to the Council, May 18, 1757, *DHSM*, 13:66, 66–67.
79. Pownall to Lithgow, January 21, 1758; Lithgow to Pownall, February 16, 1758, *DHSM*, 13:121–22, 125; Resolves, January 25, June 5, 1758, *MAR*, 16:143, 211; Paine, "Historical Sketch," November 25, 1852.

80. Whittemore, *Centennial History of Waterville*, 47; Fisher, *Fort Halifax*, 24; Resolves, January 22, 24, 25, 1758, January 18, October 6, 1759, *MAR*, 16:139, 145, 263, 398.
81. Anderson, *Crucible of War*, 297–386; "CHARLES-TOWN, September 29," *South Carolina Gazette*, September 22–29, 1759.
82. "Advertisement. The Proprietors of the Kennebeck Purchase," Plymouth Company Records, Maine Historical Society, Coll. 60, Box 13, Folder 5; "Advertisement. The Proprietors of the Kennebeck Purchase," *Boston Post-Boy*, February 24, 1760.
83. Hopkins, "The Lithgow Family," 7; Goold, "Fort Halifax," 283.
84. "BOSTON, August 23," *Pennsylvania Gazette*, September 10, 1761; Montresor, "Journal of an Expedition in 1760."
85. Montresor, "Montresor's Journal," 460; BOSTON, October 19," *Pennsylvania Gazette*, October 29, 1761.
86. Bernard to the Earl of Halifax, November 9, 1764, *DHSM*, 13:390; Muster Roll, Joseph Chadwick, 1764; Nathan Jones, 1764, Massachusetts Archives, 99:285, 295.
87. Paine, "Historical Sketch," November 11, 25, 1852; "Newspaper Clippings by Paine," 12.
88. Patterson, "Marriages from Lincoln County Records," 136.
89. Mitchell and Davis, *Winslow Register*, 23, 30–31; Winslow Comprehensive Planning Committee, *Comprehensive Plan*, 2.
90. Bernard, Message to the House, June 5, 1764; Lithgow to Bernard, April 16, 1766, *DHSM*, 13:342–43, 14:133; Extract of Lithgow to Gardiner, March 26, 1764, Massachusetts Archives, 33:294.
91. "BOSTON, January 6," "PORTSMOUTH, September 4," *Pennsylvania Gazette*, January 30, September 18, 1766; Fisher, *Fort Halifax*, 20.
92. Fisher, *Fort Halifax*, 20; Printed Proclamation of Governor Francis Bernard, April 14, 1766, Massachusetts Archives, 33:379; Lithgow to Bernard, April 14, 16, May 28, 1766, *DHSM*, 14:130–32, 133, 137-38; Council Minutes and Francis Bernard, Proclamation, April 30, 1766, Massachusetts Archives, 33:378–79, 380.
93. J. Flagg to Bernard, August 20, 1767, *DHSM*, 14:146–47; Muster Roll, William Lithgow, 1754–56, Massachusetts Archives, 94:245.
94. Francis Bernard, "Massachusetts Bay Report," 1763, 12; Fisher, *Fort Halifax*, 22–23; *Journals of the House of Representatives of Massachusetts*, 43:120 (June 24, 1766); Hopkins, "The Lithgow Family," 6; Muster Roll, William Lithgow, 1766–67, Massachusetts Archives, 99:363.
95. Goold, "Fort Halifax," 286–88.
96. Mitchell and Davis, *Winslow Register*, 22.

Chapter 4

97. Coolidge and Smith, *Colonial Entrepreneur*; Gardiner to McKechnie, April 6, 1775, Massachusetts Archives, 196:237; Ulrich, *A Midwife's Tale*, 14, 16, 369–70; Fisher, *Fort Halifax*, 24.
98. Goold, "Fort Halifax," 288; Kingsbury, "Town of Winslow," 550; Beedy, *Mothers of Maine*, 68.
99. Mitchell and Davis, *Winslow Register*, 25; Resolve, April 26, 1771, *MAR*, 5:136–37; Goold, "Fort Halifax," 288.
100. "Fort Halifax Oldest Wooden Block House in America," *Morning Sentinel*, April 24, 1971; Winslow Town Minutes, 1772, 3; 1775, 12.
101. Scalisi and Ryan, "Peter Pattee," 73–75; Kingsbury, "Town of Winslow," 541, 546, 550.
102. "QUEBEC, September 19," *Pennsylvania Gazette*, October 13, 1773.
103. Winslow Town Minutes, 1774, 8, 10.
104. Henry, *Account of Arnold's Campaign against Quebec*, 16, 18; Winslow Town Minutes, 1775, 12; Desjardins, *Through a Howling Wilderness*, 55–57.
105. Senter, *Journal*, 15–16; Benedict Arnold to Captain Farnsworth, September 29, 1775, Maine Memory Network #1280, http://www.mainememory.net/media/pdf/1280.pdf; Meigs, *Journal*, 11; Goold, "Fort Halifax," 277.
106. Darley, *Voices from a Wilderness Expedition*, 104, 105, 127, 134, 153; "Arnold Expedition Historical Society."
107. Desjardins, *Through a Howling Wilderness*, 200–2.
108. Paine, "Historical Sketch," November 25, 1852; Goold, "Fort Halifax," 277–78; Horne, *Winslow*, 87.
109. Selectmen and Council of Safety for Winslow to Bowdoin, February 14, 1777; Pattee to Bowdoin, February 16, 1777, *DHSM*, 14:407–9, 409–10; Resolve, February 1, 1777, *MAR*, 19:793; Ulrich, *A Midwife's Tale*, 14, 16, 369–70.
110. MacDougall, *Penobscot Dance of Resistance*, 104–5; Cushing to the Massachusetts Council, October 18, 1779, Massachusetts Archives, 201:370; "Gen. Peleg Wadsworth. Mr. Goold's Paper Before the Historical Society," *Portland Daily Press*, March 1, 1882; Marriner, Little Talks #1166, May 21, 1978, http://web.colby.edu/specialcollections/2011/02/22/lt1166-readonly.
111. Tarkson to Powell, August 28, 1779; Cushing, Report, October 18, 1779, *DHSM*, 17:57, 390–92; Resolves, September 27, October 5, 1779, *MAR*, 21:160–61, 194; MacDougall, *Penobscot Dance of Resistance*, 104.
112. Petition of Penobscot Chiefs [ca. October 30, 1780]; Resolves, October 30, 31; Report, November 4, 1780, *DHSM*, 19:6–8, 8–9, 15–16; Resolves, November 6, 11, 1780, July 6, 1781, *MAR*, 21:139, 151, 667–68; MacDougall, *Penobscot Dance of Resistance*, 104.

113. Certificate, June 26, 1781; J. Brewer to Devens, September 14, 1781, October 4, 1782; J. Brewer to Hancock, September 15, 1783, *DHSM*, 19:297, 319–20, 20:105–7, 261–62, Paine, "Historical Sketch," November 11, 25, 1852; "Newspaper Clippings by Paine," 11.
114. "Complaint of Juniper Berthiaume," November 20, 1781; J. Brewer to Devens, May 6, 1782, *DHSM*, 19:373, 20:10–11.
115. Pattee to Hancock, August 10, 1782; Lithgow to Hancock, August 13, 1782; Berthiaume to Hancock, [late September 1782]; "Memorial of Eastern Indians to Governor Hancock," August 27, 1782; Resolve, October 17, 1782, June 4, 1783, *DHSM*, 20:67–68, 68–71, 81–82, 232–33.
116. Resolve, November 6, 1782, *MAR*, 22:298; in Senate, September 30, 1782; Report and Resolve on Petition, October 17 and November 6, 1782; Petition Josiah Brewer, October 17, 1783; Account Josiah Brewster, October 31, 1783, *DHSM*, 20:82–83, 111–12, 273–74, 274–75.
117. Petition of Josiah Brewer, October 22, 1783; Resolve, March 2, 1784, *DHSM*, 20:308, 315.
118. Fisher, *Fort Halifax*, 24; "Robert Hallowell Gardiner," in Hatch, *Maine: A History*, 340–41.
119. Resolve, October 4, 1780, *MAR*, 20:655; Kershaw, *Kennebeck Proprietors*, 287; Whittemore, *History of Waterville*, 114.

Chapter 5

120. Paine, "Historical Sketch," November 4, 11, 25, 1852; Mitchell and Davis, *Winslow Register*, 22, 47–48.
121. Kingsbury, "Town of Winslow," 546; Paine, "Historical Sketch," November 18, 25, 1852; Scalisi and Ryan, "Peter Pattee," 73–75.
122. "Village of Indians Extended Along Banks of Sebasticook, Town Was Incorporated in April of Year 1771," *Morning Sentinel*, April 24, 1971.
123. Fisher, *History of Clinton*, 287–89; Marriner, Little Talks #1150, http://web.colby.edu/specialcollections/2011/02/21/lt1150-readonly.
124. Marriner, Little Talks #1150.
125. Kendall, *Travels*, 3:49.
126. "Newspaper Clippings by Paine," 2.
127. Carter, *Discovery of a Grandmother*, 153–54.
128. Chipman, *General Catalogue*, 32.
129. Carter, *Discovery of a Grandmother*, 153–54, 160.
130. Paine, *Paine Genealogy*, 141–43; Marriner, Little Talks #1202, May 6, 1979, http://web.colby.edu/specialcollections/2011/02/22/lt1202-readonly; "Colby Writers," *Colby Echo*, October 13, 1920.
131. Paine, *Paine Genealogy*, 142.

132. Paine, "Historical Sketch," November 4, 11, 1852.
133. Ibid., November 4, 1852.
134. Ibid., November 18, 1852.
135. Ibid.; "Newspaper Clippings by Paine," 7.
136. Ibid., 8; Paine, "Historical Sketch," November 18, 25, 1852.
137. John Richards to Hiram Simpson, March 13, 1855, Deed; Hiram Simpson to Asa Redington [Jr.], November 21, 1856, Deed, KCRD, Book 197, 480–81; Book 259, 412–13.
138. Marriner, Little Talks #95, February 4, 1951, http://web.colby.edu/specialcollections/2010/11/21/lt095-readonly.
139. Gilman to Willis, February 2, 1870, Curatorial Files, Maine Historical Society, A86–895.
140. "Vandalism," *Waterville Mail*, April 19, 1867; Cranmer, "Blockhouses and Cellars," 4–5.
141. "Messrs. Editors," "Fort Halifax," *Waterville Mail*, December 6, 1867; April 18, 1873; Asa Redington [Jr.] to Ticonic Water Power Company, Deed, August 30, 1867, KCRD, Book 262, 381.
142. "The Pullman Palace Car Excursion," *Portsmouth Journal of Literature and Politics*, May 20, 1871.
143. "The Palace Car Excursion!," *Portland Daily Press*, May 19, 1871.
144. "Fort Halifax," *Waterville Mail*, April 18, 1873.
145. Chipman, *General Catalogue*, 209, 272; Mitchell and Davis, *Winslow Register*, 31; Winslow Town Minutes, March 9, 1874; Whittemore, *Centennial History of Waterville*, 94; Kingsbury, "Town of Winslow," 554, 565.
146. *Portland Daily Press*, April 21, 1873.
147. "Notes," *Maine Farmer*, March 30, 1882.
148. Kingsbury, "Town of Winslow," 541; Ticonic Water Power Company to Lockwood Company, Deed, April 9, 1875, KCRD, Book 298, 438.
149. "The Story of the Old Block House (Continued)," *Waterville Mail*, March 27, 1874; "Newspaper Clippings by Paine," 13.
150. Goold, "William Goold"; "City News and Gossip," *Maine Farmer*, December 4, 1875.
151. Goold, "Fort Halifax," 199.
152. *Portland Daily Press*, March 31, 1876.
153. *Colby Echo*, June 1, 1879.
154. Wilson, "Indian Relics"; *Waterville Mail*, February 15, 1884.

CHAPTER 6

155. "A Famous Maine Fortification," *Lewiston Evening Journal*, April 24, 1897.
156. "Fort Halifax," *Colby Echo*, April 29, 1893.

157. Charles A. Allen, "Old Fort Halifax," *Forest and Stream*, October 1906.
158. "Fort Halifax," *Colby Echo*, April 29, 1893.
159. Horne, *Winslow*, 484–87; Mitchell and Davis, *Winslow Register*, 44–45; Winslow Comprehensive Planning Committee, *Comprehensive Plan*, 2, 52.
160. "Block House at Fort Halifax. As It Now Stands in Winslow," *Bangor Daily Commercial*, September 22, 1900; "Book Review," *Colby Echo*, October 5, 1900.
161. Lockwood Company to Maine Central Railroad Company, Deed, August 25, 1902, KCRD, Book 442, 267; "Fort Halifax Block House Given Over to Daughters," *Waterville Morning Sentinel*, June 3, 1924.
162. "Used Snow," *Boston Daily Globe*, January 7, 1905.
163. Mary Howard, "Things I Remember about the Early Days of Fort Halifax Chapter, D.A.R.," 1973, 1–3, Fort Halifax Chapter, DAR, Scrapbooks; Carter, *Discovery of a Grandmother*, 40; *Daughters of the American Revolution Magazine*, 1957, 636; "Fort Halifax Chapter. Daughters of American Revolution Organize in Winslow," *Waterville Morning Sentinel*, March 18, 1913; Hope Wixson, "Fort Halifax Is Given to Maine Park Board," *Morning Sentinel*, November 1, 1965.
164. *Colby Echo*, May 6, 1914.
165. Jennie Howard, "History of Winslow as Read by Miss Jennie Paine Howard," *Morning Sentinel*, May 24, 1921; Chipman, *General Catalogue*, 347.
166. Alexander Baird, "Fort Halifax," *Periscope*, 1922, 6, Winslow Public Library.
167. Howard, "Things I Remember," 4–5; Maine Central Railroad Company to Fort Halifax Chapter, Daughters of the American Revolution, Deed, May 20, 1924, KCRD, Book 615, 563–65.
168. "Fort Halifax Blockhouse Given Over to Daughters," *Waterville Morning Sentinel*, June 3, 1924; Minnie Garland, "History of Fort Halifax," [1954], 2–3, in Hope Wixson DAR Papers, Winslow Public Library.
169. Garland, "History of Fort Halifax," 3; Howard, "Things I Remember," 4–5.
170. Yetta H. Russakoff to Norman G. Woodbury, Deed, August 8, 1943; Cyr Brothers Company to Norman G. Woodbury, Deed, November 12, 1943; Jefferson C. Smith to Peter Calzolari, Deed, September 16, 1944, KCRD, Book 1325, 379–80, 375–76, Book 813, 226–28.
171. "Cameraman Catches Maine Flood Scenes as Major Rivers Reach Peak Flow," *Waterville Morning Sentinel*, March 23, 1936; "Fort Halifax, U.S. Route 201, Winslow, Kennebec County, ME," http://www.loc.gov/pictures/item/me0062.
172. Mabel Demers, Minnie Garland, and Charlotte Norton, undated report, Hope Wixson DAR Papers, Winslow Public Library; The Texas Company v. Capitol Distributors, Court Document, July 26, 1945, KCRD, Book 819, 441.
173. Jack Nivison and Stan Mathieu, interview, June 23, 2013.

174. Hope Wixson, "Fort Halifax Is Given To Maine Park Board," *Morning Sentinel*, November 1, 1965; *Proceedings of the Continental Congress of the National Society of the Daughters of the American Revolution*, 1948, 164.
175. "Three Charter Members Fort Halifax Chapter, DAR, To Be in Costume"; "DAR Will Re-dedicate Fort Halifax Today," "Colorful Fort Halifax Re-dedication Marks Maine DAR Session Here," *Waterville Morning Sentinel*, July 20, 21, 1954; "Fort Halifax Rededicated By State DAR Officials," *Lewiston Evening Journal*, July 22, 1954.
176. "Gift Flagpole Dedicated, Fort Halifax DAR," *Waterville Morning Sentinel*, June 13, 1956; Hope Wixson to Mr. and Mrs. Donald Corbett, July 10, 1956, Fort Halifax Chapter, DAR, Scrapbooks.
177. "Final Surfacing Won't Be Put on Bridge Until Next Spring," *Waterville Morning Sentinel*, November 9, 1959; State of Maine, Resolve, H.P. 136, L.D. 199, February 15, 1961, in Hope Wixson DAR Papers, Winslow Public Library.
178. Hope Wixson, "Fort Halifax Praised by Visiting Experts," *Morning Sentinel*, August 28, 1962.
179. *Colby Echo*, October 16, 1964.
180. "Hope Wixson, "Fort Halifax Is Given To Maine Park Board," *Morning Sentinel*, November 1, 1965; "Fort Halifax DAR Hears Supervisor of Historic Sites," *Maine Sunday Telegram*, February 20, 1966.
181. Fort Halifax Chapter, DAR, to State of Maine, Deed, January 19, 1966; Bill's Oil Service to Town of Winslow, Deed, November 15, 1967, KCRD, Book 1408, 369–70; Book 1458, 170–72; Rettig, "National Register of Historic Places Inventory Nomination Form."
182. Winslow Comprehensive Planning Committee, *Comprehensive Plan*, 2.
183. Ibid., 15; Marriner, Little Talks #57, February 26, 1950, http://web.colby.edu/specialcollections/2010/11/12/lt057-readonly.

CHAPTER 7

184. Constance Bolduc, "Fort Halifax Project Discussed by Winslow Historical Society," *Morning Sentinel*, August 12, 1970; Pearley Lachance, interview, October 23, 2013; Council Minutes, January 12, 1970; August 31, September 13, 1971; November 20, December 11, 1972; Robert R. LaRochelle, "Report of the Town Council Chairman," *Annual Report, 1970*, 6, *1973*, 6–7.
185. Clark, *Status of Fort Halifax Park*; "Old Fort Halifax Site May Be Recreational Area," *Central Maine Morning Sentinel*, November 19, 1974; Steve Clark, interview, November 10, 2013.

186. Sarah Betts, "Arnold Doughty 600 Invading Central Maine," *Central Maine Morning Sentinel*, September 24, 1975.
187. Paul Betit, "AEQ-75 Bucks Rain, Heads Toward Augusta," *Central Maine Morning Sentinel*, September 27, 1975.
188. Sarah Betts, "Neither Rain Nor Mud Dismays Latter-Day Patriots," *Central Maine Morning Sentinel*, September 29, 1975.
189. Sarah Betts, "200 Years of History Tug City's Heartstrings," *Central Maine Morning Sentinel*, September 29, 1975.
190. Ann McGowan, "It's On To Quebec! Arnold's Men Visit Madison, Solon, Kingfield and Stratton," *Central Maine Morning Sentinel*, September 30, 1975.
191. Ernest Baker, "Bicentennial Commission," *Annual Report, 1976*, 23.
192. Council Minutes, April 26, May 10, 1976; Norman G. Woodbury to Town of Winslow, Deed, November 22, 1976, KCRD, Book 1967, 285–86.
193. Elliott Potter, "Winslow Fort Gets a Face-Lift," *Central Maine Morning Sentinel*, October 3, 1977.
194. Council Minutes, May 9, August 12, 1977, January 9, 30, 1978; Capitol Distributors to LeBaron [Lee] Spaulding and Norman G. Poulin, Mortgage, June 28, 1979; Deed, June 28, 1979, KCRD, Book 2219, 113–15, 158–60.
195. Robert R. LaRochelle, "Report of the Town Council Chairman," *Annual Report, 1975*, 7; Jeff Wuorio, "Fort Halifax to Be Focal Point of New Winslow Park Area," *Central Maine Morning Sentinel*, September 19, 1980.
196. "Development of Ft. Halifax Site Discussed by VFW Post," *Central Maine Morning Sentinel*, September 7, 1979.
197. Philip Norvish, "Anniversary Speaker Urges Clean Up of Fort Halifax," *Central Maine Morning Sentinel*, October 1, 1979.
198. Larry Rosenthal, "Winslow to Mark Ft. Halifax Anniversary"; "Winslow Gets $2500 For Ft. Halifax Work"; Terri Stanley, "Dedication in August," *Central Maine Morning Sentinel*, September 25, November 9, 1979; July 29, 1981; Leonel Breton, "Parks and Recreation Department," *Annual Report 1979–1980*, 15; David H. Blair, "Town Council Report," *Annual Report, 1980–1981*, 7, 16.
199. "Picnic Tables Ready," and Terri Stanley, "Pioneers: Young workers create Fort Halifax Park," *Central Maine Morning Sentinel*, April 15, July 29, 1981; Leonel A. Breton, "Parks & Recreation Department," *Annual Report, 1981–1982*, 13; Jack Nivison, interview, August 7, 2013.
200. Stanley, "Dedication in August," "Winslow History Enshrined," *Central Maine Morning Sentinel*, August 31, 1981.
201. Leonel A. Breton, "Parks and Recreation Department," *Annual Report 1981–1982*, 13.
202. Council Minutes, November 8, 1982; LeBaron [Lee] Spaulding and Norman G. Poulin to Town of Winslow, Deed, January 5, 1983, KCRD, Book 2537, 66; Lee Spaulding, interview, November 24, 2013;

203. Town Manager's Report, February 8, 1984, in Council Minutes, February 13, 1984; "Demolition Day," "Spring Flooding," *Central Maine Morning Sentinel*, March 21, August 24, 1984; Leonel Breton, "Parks and Recreation Dept. Report," "Parks & Recreation Dept. Report," *Annual Report 1985*, 23; *1986*, 25.
204. Leonel A. Breton, "Parks and Recreation Department," *Annual Report 1981–1982*, 13; *1982–1983*, 13; Pearley Lachance, interview, October 23, 2013.

CHAPTER 8

205. *Colby Echo*, April 2, 1987; Jack Nivison, interview, August 7, 2013.
206. Sheila McDonald, "Fort Halifax: Recovery of a National Landmark," *Kennebec Proprietor*, Fall 1987, 15; Jack Nivison, interview, August 7, 2013.
207. Gerry Boyle, "Kennebec Washes Away 200 Years of History," *Central Maine Morning Sentinel*, April 10, 1987.
208. Bob Woodbury, "Winslow Fort Still Missing," *Central Maine Morning Sentinel*, April 4, 1987; Keith Edwards, "Parts of Fort Halifax Possibly Uncovered at Richmond Dig Site," *Morning Sentinel*, June 5, 2013.
209. Boyle, "Kennebec Washes Away 200 Years."
210. Marie Howard, "Fort Halifax plaque found on Casco Bay Island," *Central Maine Morning Sentinel*, July 14, 1987.
211. Bob Keyes, "Archaeological Dig Set at Ft. Halifax," *Central Maine Morning Sentinel*, May 23, 1987.
212. Herb Hartman to Don Carter, April 19, 1988, Friends of Fort Halifax Collection.
213. Bob Keyes, "State Ponders Restoration of Fort as Pieces Surface," *Central Maine Morning Sentinel*, April 10, 1987.
214. Peter Blais, "Fort Halifax Restoration Funds Swelled," *Central Maine Morning Sentinel*, August 6, 1987.
215. McDonald, "Fort Halifax."
216. Peter Blais, "Crew Digs in at Fort Halifax," *Central Maine Morning Sentinel*, August 18, 1987; McDonald, "Fort Halifax"; Lee Cranmer and Anne Hilton, "It Stood Its Ground Until…: The Archaeological Excavations at Fort Halifax," *Kennebec Proprietor*, Fall 1987, 15–17, 21–24; John Messeder, "Archaeologists Fix Site of First Fort Halifax," *Bangor Daily News*, October 27, 1987.
217. Mary Grow, "Archaeological Dig Gives Clues about Old Trading Post," Susan Davis, "Fort Halifax 234-Year-Old Landmark Reborn," *Central Maine Morning Sentinel*, May 23, October 29, 1988.
218. Stan Mathieu to Dale Doughty, "Reconstruction of Fort Halifax, Winslow, Maine," [April 1987], Friends of Fort Halifax Collection.

219. Elliot Potter, "Blockhouse Builder Played in Fort as a Kid: Stan Mathieu Found It Was a Labor of Love," *Central Maine Morning Sentinel*, October 29, 1988.
220. Victoria Hershey, "Local Man Nails Ft. Halifax Rebuilding Job," *Central Maine Morning Sentinel*, January 7, 1988.
221. Stan Mathieu, interview, June 20, 2013.
222. Anthony F. Cristan, "History Found Piece by Piece at Fort Halifax Dig," Mary Grow, "Archaeological Dig Gives Clues about Old Trading Post," *Central Maine Morning Sentinel*, May 7, May 23, 1988.
223. Kim Leighton, "Prehistoric Ft. Halifax Served Indians as Local Fish Store," *Central Maine Morning Sentinel*, April 25, 1989.
224. Marianne E. Hobert, "Fort Halifax Blockhouse: Unique Foundation Can Survive Flood," *Maine Sunday Telegram*, February 19, 1989.
225. Anthony Cristan, "It's Back Through Time to Days of Old," *Central Maine Morning Sentinel*, July 29, 1988.
226. *Reconstruction of Fort Halifax* video, Winslow Public Library.
227. Stan Mathieu, interview, June 20, 2013.
228. "Fort Halifax Membership Drive Opens," *Central Maine Morning Sentinel*, July 29, 1988; Rudy Fougere, interview, July 26, 2013.
229. Anthony F. Cristan, "Winslow Celebrates Its Past as They Rebuild the Symbol," *Central Maine Morning Sentinel*, August 1, 1988.
230. Cranmer, "Blockhouses and Cellars"; "Fort Halifax dig," *Central Maine Morning Sentinel*, October 4, 1989.
231. *Reconstruction of Fort Halifax*.
232. Earle Shettleworth Jr. to Katherine H. Stevenson, March 2, 1989, Friends of Fort Halifax Collection.
233. Fort Halifax Rededication Program, October 30, 1988, Friends of Fort Halifax Collection.
234. Sharon Mack, "Reconstructed Fort Halifax blockhouse dedicated," *Bangor Daily News*, October 31, 1988.
235. Kim Leighton, "Rebuilt Fort Halifax Faces Decertification," *Central Maine Morning Sentinel*, July 22–23, 1989.
236. Maine Historic Preservation Commission, et. al, "Fort Halifax National Historic Landmark Winslow Maine: Preliminary Master Plan," August 1989, Earle Shettleworth Jr. to Donald V. Carter, August 22, 1989; Friends of Fort Halifax Collection.
237. Donald V. Carter to Dick Kelso, August 1, 1989; Herb Hartman to Donald V. Carter, August 29, 1989; Ed Bearss to Associate Director, Cultural Resources, September 12, 1989: Inspection of Fort Halifax and Proposed De-designation Study, August 23–24, 1989, Friends of Fort Halifax Collection.
238. Donald V. Carter to Edwin C. Bearss, August 10, 1989, Friends of Fort Halifax Collection.

CHAPTER 9

239. Daniel L. Austin, "Rain doesn't stop Gen. Winslow," *Central Maine Morning Sentinel*, July 26, 1990; Program: Fort Halifax Days, 1990, Friends of Fort Halifax Collection.
240. Maine Historic Preservation Commission, et. al., "Fort Halifax Preliminary Master Plan."
241. "Winslow Family Fourth of July Celebration," http://www.winslow4thofjuly.com.
242. Ed Welch, "Fort Halifax Memorabilia," *Town Line*, December 13, 1993.
243. Cranmer, "Blockhouses and Cellars"; Fred Davis, "Fort Halifax Dig," *Town Line*, December 2, 1991; Daniel Austin, "Ancient Artifacts Unearthed," *Central Maine Morning Sentinel*, August 24, 1994; *CNEHA Newsletter*, July 1995, 6.
244. Winslow Comprehensive Planning Committee, *Comprehensive Plan*, 2.
245. Clark, *Status of Fort Halifax Park*.
246. "Development of Ft. Halifax Site Discussed By VFW Post," "Dedication in August," "Winslow History Enshrined," *Central Maine Morning Sentinel*, September 7, 1979; July 29, 1981; August 31, 1981; Council Minutes, June 10, 1985.
247. Fort Halifax Park Planning Committee and Terrence J. DeWan & Associates, *Fort Halifax Park Concept Master Plan*, 2, 4; Amy Bell Segal, interview, September 24, 2013.
248. Larry Grard, "Rain Delays Action at Fort Halifax," *Morning Sentinel*, June 20, 2004.
249. Council Minutes, March 14, April 11, May 9, 2005.
250. Ibid., November 22, 2005; John Giroux, interview, November 23, 2013.
251. "Some Accomplishments," May 15, 2007, Friends of Fort Halifax Collection.
252. Friends of Fort Halifax minutes, October 10, 2007, Friends of Fort Halifax Collection.
253. Winslow Comprehensive Planning Committee, *Comprehensive Plan*, ii, 11, 12.
254. Winslow's Fourth of July Committee, *Fort Halifax Park*, 2.
255. Ibid., 8, 12, 13, 24.
256. Council Minutes, March 24, 31, 2010, Friends of Fort Halifax Collection; Scott Monroe, "Upgrades to Fort Halifax Park Have Some Residents Concerned"; "Mr. Fourth of July Stepping Aside at Top of His Game"; "Free Outdoor Movie Series in Park to Start in Winslow," *Morning Sentinel*, May 24, June 10, July 13, 2010.
257. Friends of Fort Halifax, *A Confluence of Cultures*, 2, 7, 11, 13.
258. Doug Harlow, "Boy Rescued from River: Legally Blind Man Guides Winslow 9-Year-Old to Shore," *Morning Sentinel*, June 16, 2004.

259. Anonymous, "Fort Halifax Park Friends Have Misplaced Priorities," *Morning Sentinel*, February 4, 2010; Minutes, July 15, 2010, Friends of Fort Halifax Collection.
260. Scott Monroe, "Fort Halifax Park Peace Talks Begin"; "Fort Halifax Blockhouse to Open again in Winslow," *Morning Sentinel*, July 21, 2010; April 18, 2011; Fort Halifax Park Planning Committee and Terrence J. DeWan & Associates, *Fort Halifax Park Concept Master Plan*.
261. Ibid., i, 1, 4.
262. Fort Halifax Park Implementation Committee Minutes, 2011–14.

Conclusion

263. Scott Monroe, "Waterville Wayward Seal Rescued," *Morning Sentinel*, November 29, 2008.
264. Ibid.
265. Scott Monroe, "Wayward Seal Well on Way to Freedom," *Morning Sentinel*, December 20, 2008.
266. Dwayne Rioux, "Striped Bass Have Arrived," *Morning Sentinel*, May 23, 2001; "The Sebasticook Watershed."
267. "Winslow Family Fourth of July Celebration."
268. Dennis Dacus, "Winslow Parks and Recreation Report," *Annual Report, 2010–2011*, 22.
269. "A View from Fort Hill," *Waterville Mail*, June 24, 1881.

Bibliography

Newspapers and Magazines

Bangor Daily Commercial, *Bangor Daily News*, *Boston Daily Globe*, *Boston Gazette*, *Boston Post-Boy*, *Central Maine Morning Sentinel*, *Colby Echo*, *Council for Northeast Historical Archaeology* [*CNEHA*] *Newsletter*, *Daughters of the American Revolution Magazine*, *Eastern Mail*, *Forest and Stream*, *Kennebec Journal*, *Kennebec Proprietor*, *Lewiston Journal Magazine*, *Maine Farmer*, *Morning Sentinel*, *Maine Sunday Telegram*, *Pennsylvania Gazette*, *Portland Daily Press*, *Portsmouth Journal of Literature and Politics*, *Proceedings of the Continental Congress of the National Society of the Daughters of the American Revolution*, *Town Line*, *Waterville Mail*, *Waterville Morning Sentinel*.

Archival Sources and Digital Resources

Colby College Miller Library, Special Collections
Marriner, Ernest. "Little Talks on Common Things." http://web.colby.edu/csc-marriner.

Commonwealth of Massachusetts, Archives Division, Boston
Massachusetts Archives. Microfilm at Maine State Library, Augusta, ME.

Fort Halifax Chapter, Daughters of the American Revolution, privately held.
Scrapbooks

Friends of Fort Halifax Collection, privately held.
Correspondence, 1987–1990
Meeting Minutes, 2005–2013

Kennebec County Registry of Deeds [KCRD], https://gov.propertyinfo.com/me-kennebec.
Land Records, 1799–2014

Maine Historical Society, Portland, ME
Curatorial Files
Maine Memory Network, http://www.mainememory.net.
Newspaper Clippings by Paine on the History of Fort Halifax in Winslow, Maine, 1852, Coll. 1255.
Plymouth Company (1749–1816), Records, ca. 1625–1824, Coll. 60.
Morning Sentinel Headquarters, Waterville, ME
Photographic Archives and Research Files
William L. Clements Library, University of Michigan, Ann Arbor
Bernard, Francis. "Massachusetts Bay Report." 1763.
Fort Halifax and the Kennebec River: Quebec July 25th, 1761. Map.
Winslow Public Library, Winslow, ME
Hope Wixson DAR Papers
The Reconstruction of Fort Halifax. Videocassette, 1988.
Winslow Vertical Files
Winslow Town Office Building, Winslow, ME
Fort Halifax Park Implementation Committee Minutes, 2011–2014
Winslow Town Minutes and Council Minutes, 1771–2012

Published Primary Sources

Barber, John. "Journal of Capt. Eleazer Melvin's Company, Shirley's Expedition, 1754." *New England Historical and Genealogical Register* 27 (July 1873): 281–85.

Baxter, James Phinney, ed. *Documentary History of the State of Maine* [*DHSM*]. 24 vols. Portland: Maine Historical Society, 1869–1916.

Carter, Lydia Augusta Paine. *The Discovery of a Grandmother: Glimpses into the Homes and Lives of Eight Generations of an Ipswich-Paine Family*. Newtonville, MA: H.H. Carter, 1920.

Clark, Steve. *Status of Fort Halifax Park and Historical Site Project*. Winslow, ME, 1974.

Darley, Stephen. *Voices from a Wilderness Expedition: The Journals and Men of Benedict Arnold's Expedition to Quebec in 1775*. Bloomington, IN: AuthorHouse, 2011.

DeWan & Associates, Terrence J. *Fort Halifax Park*. Falmouth, ME, 2002.

Fort Halifax Park Planning Committee and Terrence J. DeWan & Associates. "Fort Halifax Park Concept Master Plan." June 2011. http://www.winslow-me.gov/content/1359149616fort-halifax-park-adopted-plan-07-11-2011-web2.pdf (accessed February 1, 2014).

Friends of Fort Halifax. *A Confluence of Cultures: Fort Halifax Park Concept Map* (July 2010). Winslow, ME, 2010.

"From Boston News Letter, 26th Sept., 1754." *New England Historical and Genealogical Register* 13 (April 1859): 174.

Hakluyt, Richard, and Samuel Purchas. *Hakluytus Posthumus or Purchas His Pilgrimes, Containing a History of the World in Sea Voyages and Lande Travells.* 4 vols. 1625. Reprint, 20 vols. Published for the Hakluyt Society at the University Press, 1905–1907.

Henry, John Joseph. *Account of Arnold's Campaign against Quebec, and of the Hardships and Sufferings of that Band of Heroes.* Albany, NY: Joel Munsell, 1877.

Kendall, Edward Augustus. *Travels Through the Northern Parts of the United States, in the Years 1807 and 1808.* 3 vols. New York: I. Riley, 1809.

Maine Historic Preservation Commission, Maine Bureau of Parks and Recreation, Friends of Fort Halifax, Town of Winslow, Maine. "Fort Halifax National Historic Landmark Winslow, Maine: Preliminary Master Plan." Augusta, ME, 1989.

Massachusetts. *The Acts and Resolves, Public and Private of the Province of Massachusetts Bay* [*MAR*]. 21 vols. Boston: Wright & Potter Printing Co., 1869–1922.

———. *Journals of the House of Representatives of Massachusetts* [1715–1779]. 55 Vols. Boston: Massachusetts Historical Society, 1919–1990.

Meigs, Return J. *Journal of the Expedition against Quebec Under Command of Col. Benedict Arnold, in the Year 1775.* New York: privately printed, 1864.

Montresor, John. "Lt. John Montresor's Journal of an Expedition in 1760 Across Maine from Quebec." Edited by G. D. Scull. *New England Historical and Genealogical Register* 36 (January 1882): 29–36.

———. *Montresor's Journal.* Edited by the Maine Historical Society. Collections of the Maine Historical Society, Vol. I. Portland, ME: Bailey & Noyes, 1865.

Patterson, William D., ed. "Marriages from Lincoln County Records." *Maine Historical Magazine* 9 (1894): 135–43.

Senter, Isaac. *The Journal of Isaac Senter.* Philadelphia: Historical Society of Pennsylvania, 1846.

Shettleworth, Earle G., Jr. *Waterville.* Charleston, SC: Arcadia Publishing, 2013.

Shirley, William. *Correspondence of William Shirley, Governor of Massachusetts and Military Commander in America, 1731–1760.* 2 vols. Edited by Charles Henry Lincoln. New York: Macmillan, 1912.

Williamson, Joseph. "Materials for a History of Fort Halifax." Collections of the Maine Historical Society, Vol. VII. Portland, ME: Bailey & Noyes, 1876.

Winslow Comprehensive Planning Committee. "Town of Winslow Comprehensive Plan Final Draft." November 2008. Winslow, ME, 2008.

Winslow Fourth of July Committee. "Fort Halifax Park: New Proposed Schematic Master Plan, 2009–2010." Winslow, ME, 2010.

Secondary Sources

Allen, Charles Edwin. *History of Dresden, Maine*. Augusta, ME: Kennebec Journal Print Shop, 1931.

Anderson, Fred. *Crucible of War: The Seven Years' War and the Fate of Empire in British North America, 1754–1766*. New York: Alfred A. Knopf, 2000.

"Arnold Expedition Historical Society." http://arnoldsmarch.com/research.html (accessed February 1, 2014).

Beedy, Helen Coffin. *Mothers of Maine*. Portland, ME: Thurston Print, 1895.

Caldwell, Bill. *Rivers of Fortune: Where Maine Tides and Money Flowed*. Portland, ME: G. Gannett Pub., 1983.

Calvert, Mary. *Dawn over the Kennebec*. Lewiston, ME: Twin City Printery, 1983.

Chipman, Charles P., ed. *General Catalogue of Officers, Graduates and Former Students of Colby College, 1820–1920*. Waterville, ME: Colby College, 1920.

Coolidge, Olivia E., and Danny D. Smith. *Colonial Entrepreneur: Dr. Silvester Gardiner and the Settlement of Maine's Kennebec Valley*. Gardiner, ME: Tilbury House Publishers, 1999.

Cranmer, Leon E. "Blockhouses and Cellars: The 1989 and 1990 Archaeological Work at Fort Halifax." *Maine Archaeological Society Bulletin* 31 (Fall 1991): 1–26.

———. *Cushnoc: The History and Archaeology of Plymouth Colony Traders on the Kennebec*. Augusta: Maine Archaeological Society, 1990.

———. "Fort Halifax Archaeological Excavations 1991." *Maine Archaeological Society Bulletin* 33 (Fall 1993): 23–31.

Desjardin, Thomas A. *Through a Howling Wilderness: Benedict Arnold's March to Quebec, 1775*. New York: St. Martin's Press, 2006.

De Watteville, Herman Gaston. *The British Soldier: His Daily Life from Tudor to Modern Times*. New York: Putnam, 1955.

Dow, George Francis. *Fort Western on the Kennebec: The Story of Its Construction in 1754 and What Happened There*. Augusta, ME: Gannett Publishing Company, 1922.

Fisher, Carleton E. *History of Clinton, Maine*. Augusta, ME: K.J. Printing, 1970.

———. *History of Fort Halifax*. Winthrop, ME: printed by Courier-Gazette, 1972.

"Fort Halifax, U.S. Route 201, Winslow, Kennebec County, ME." http://www.loc.gov/pictures/item/me0062 (accessed February 1, 2014).

Fuller, B.A.G. "Fort Halifax." *Maine Genealogist and Biographer* 2 (December 1876): 51–53.

Goold, Nathan. "William Goold." *Collections and Proceedings of the Maine Historical Society*. 2nd Series, Vol. IX. Portland, ME: Maine Historical Society, 1898.

Goold, William. "Projectors and Garrison of Fort Halifax." *Collections of the Maine Historical Society*. Vol. VIII. Portland, ME: Hoyt, Fogg, & Donham, 1881.

Hopkins, Ellen Dunlop. "The Lithgow Family." *New York Genealogical and Biographical Record* 29 (January 1898): 1–13.

Horne, Hope Braley. *Winslow: Our Town, Our People*. Winslow, ME: H.B. Horne, 1991.

Kershaw, Gordon E. *The Kennebeck Proprietors, 1749–1775*. Somersworth: New Hampshire Pub. Co., 1975.

Kingsbury, Henry D. "Town of Winslow." In *Illustrated History of Kennebec County, Maine*, edited by Henry D. Kingsbury and Simeon L. Deyo. New York: H.W. Blake & Co., 1892.

Krusell, Cynthia Hagar. *The Winslows of Careswell in Marshfield*. Revised ed. Assisted by Betty Magoun Bates. Marshfield, MA: Pondside Publishing, 2012.

MacDougall, Pauleena. *The Penobscot Dance of Resistance: Tradition in the History of a People*. Durham: University of New Hampshire Press, 2004.

Mitchell, Harry Edward, and B.V. Davis. *The Winslow Register*. Kent's Hill, ME: H.E. Mitchell Publishing Co., 1904.

Nason, Emma. *Old Colonial Houses in Maine Built Prior to 1776*. Augusta, ME: Press of the Kennebec Journal, 1908.

Paine, Albert Ware. *Paine Genealogy. Ipswich Branch*. Bangor, ME: O.F. Knowles, 1881.

Rettig, Polly M. "National Register of Historic Places Inventory—Nomination Form." http://pdfhost.focus.nps.gov/docs/NHLS/Text/68000015.pdf (accessed February 1, 2014).

———. "National Register of Historic Places Property Photograph Form." http://pdfhost.focus.nps.gov/docs/NHLS/Photos/68000015.pdf (accessed February 1, 2014).

"Robert Hallowell Gardiner." In *Maine: A History*. Vol. 4. Edited by Louis Clinton Hatch. New York: American Historical Society, 1919.

Scalisi, Marie Lollo, and Virginia M. Ryan. "Peter Pattee of Haverhill, Massachusetts: A 'Journeyman Shoemaker' and His Descendants." *New England Historical and Genealogical Magazine* 147 (1993): 73–75.

"The Sebasticook Watershed." Sebasticook Regional Land Trust. http://www.sebasticookrlt.org/where-in-the-watershed-5 (accessed February 1, 2014).

Speck, W.A. "Dunk, George Montagu, second earl of Halifax (1716–1771)." *Oxford Dictionary of National Biography*. London: Oxford University Press, 2004. Online edition available at http://www.oxforddnb.com/view/article/8266.

Thayer, Henry O. "The Lithgow Immigrants." *Sprague's Journal of Maine History* 10 (1922): 70–85.

Thurber, John. "Exhibit: Fort Halifax." Maine Memory Network. http://www.mainememory.net/bin/Features?t=fp&feat=8 (accessed February 1, 2014).

Ulrich, Laurel Thatcher. *A Midwife's Tale: The Life of Martha Ballard, Based on Her Diary, 1785–1812*. New York: Vintage, 1990.

Whittemore, Edwin Carey, ed. *The Centennial History of Waterville, Kennebec County, Maine, 1802–1902*. Waterville, ME: Executive Committee of the Centennial Celebration, 1902.

Wilson, Charles B. "Indian Relics and Encampment at Fort Halifax." *American Antiquarian, and Oriental Journal* 5 (April 1883): 181–83.

"Winslow Family Fourth of July Celebration." http://www.winslow4thofjuly.com (accessed February 1, 2014).

Winslow, Town of. *Annual Report of the Municipal Officers of the Town of Winslow. Or, Town of Winslow Maine Annual Report*. Winslow, ME, 1873– .

Interviews

Wilma Carter, Steve Clark, Dennis Dacus, Rudy Fougere, John Giroux, Barbara Healy, Mike Heavener, Elery Keene, Pearley Lachance, Roland Lessard, Stan Mathieu, Tom McCowan, Jack Nivison, JoAnn Nivison, Gerry Poissonier, Amy Bell Segal, Lee Spaulding

Index

About the Author

Daniel Tortora, PhD, is an assistant professor of history at Colby College. An expert on early American and Native American history, he speaks extensively on the French and Indian War and Revolutionary War eras, leads battlefield and historic tours and has contributed to numerous films, archaeological projects, websites, exhibits and research projects. In 2011, he was appointed to the Fort Halifax Park Implementation Committee.

Visit us at
www.historypress.net

This title is also available as an e-book